ALGEBRA – TASK & DRILL SHEETS

Principles & Standards of Math Series

Written by Nat Reed

GRADES 3 - 5

Classroom Complete Press
P.O. Box 19729
San Diego, CA 92159
Tel: 1-800-663-3609 | Fax: 1-800-663-3608
Email: service@classroomcompletepress.com

www.classroomcompletepress.com

ISBN-13: 978-1-55319-540-5

 We acknowledge the financial support of the Government of Canada through the Book Publishing Industry Development Program (BPIDP) for our publishing activities. Printed in Canada.

Process Standards Rubric

Algebra – Task & Drill Sheets

Algebra – Task Sheets

Goal	Expectations: Instructional programs from pre-kindergarten through grade 12 should enable all students to:	1	2	3	4	5	6	7	8	9	10	11	12	13	14	15	Drill Sheet 1	Drill Sheet 2	Review A	Review B	Review C
GOAL 1: Problem Solving	• build new mathematical knowledge through problem solving;	✓	✓			✓		✓	✓	✓		✓		✓	✓	✓				✓	✓
	• solve problems that arise in mathematics and in other contexts;	✓	✓			✓		✓	✓	✓		✓		✓	✓	✓				✓	✓
	• apply and adapt a variety of appropriate strategies to solve problems;	✓	✓			✓		✓		✓		✓		✓		✓				✓	✓
	• monitor and reflect on the process of mathematical problem solving.	✓	✓			✓		✓		✓		✓								✓	✓
GOAL 2: Reasoning & Proof	• recognize reasoning and proof as fundamental aspects of mathematics;	✓	✓	✓	✓	✓	✓	✓	✓	✓	✓	✓	✓	✓	✓	✓	✓	✓	✓	✓	✓
	• make and investigate mathematical conjectures;	✓	✓	✓	✓	✓	✓	✓	✓	✓	✓	✓	✓	✓	✓	✓	✓	✓	✓	✓	✓
	• develop and evaluate mathematical arguments and proofs;	✓	✓		✓			✓		✓	✓	✓	✓	✓	✓	✓	✓	✓	✓	✓	✓
	• select and use various types of reasoning and methods of proof.	✓	✓					✓		✓		✓							✓	✓	✓
GOAL 3: Communication	• organize and consolidate their mathematical thinking through communication;	✓	✓			✓		✓	✓	✓		✓				✓				✓	✓
	• communicate their mathematical thinking coherently and clearly to peers, teachers, and others;	✓	✓			✓		✓	✓	✓		✓				✓				✓	✓
	• analyze and evaluate the mathematical thinking and strategies of others;	✓	✓	✓	✓		✓	✓	✓	✓	✓	✓	✓	✓	✓	✓	✓	✓	✓	✓	✓
	• use the language of mathematics to express mathematical ideas precisely.	✓	✓	✓	✓	✓		✓	✓	✓		✓	✓		✓	✓	✓	✓	✓	✓	✓
GOAL 4: Connections	• recognize and use connections among mathematical ideas;	✓	✓	✓		✓	✓	✓	✓	✓	✓	✓	✓	✓	✓	✓	✓	✓	✓	✓	✓
	• understand how mathematical ideas interconnect and build on one another to produce a coherent whole;	✓	✓	✓		✓	✓	✓	✓	✓	✓	✓	✓	✓	✓	✓	✓	✓	✓	✓	✓
	• recognize and apply mathematics in contexts outside of mathematics.	✓	✓			✓			✓	✓		✓			✓	✓				✓	✓
GOAL 5: Representation	• create and use representations to organize, record, and communicate mathematical ideas;	✓	✓	✓	✓	✓	✓	✓	✓	✓	✓	✓	✓	✓	✓	✓	✓	✓	✓	✓	✓
	• select, apply, and translate among mathematical representations to solve problems;	✓	✓	✓		✓	✓	✓	✓	✓	✓	✓	✓	✓	✓	✓	✓	✓	✓	✓	✓
	• use representations to model and interpret physical, social, and mathematical phenomena.	✓	✓	✓		✓	✓	✓	✓	✓	✓	✓	✓	✓	✓	✓	✓	✓	✓	✓	✓

Process Standards Rubric

Algebra – Task & Drill Sheets

Algebra – Drill Sheets

Expectations: Instructional programs from pre-kindergarten through grade 12 should enable all students to:		Warm-up 1	Timed Drill 1	Timed Drill 2	Warm-up 2	Timed Drill 3	Timed Drill 4	Warm-up 3	Timed Drill 5	Timed Drill 6	Warm-up 4	Timed Drill 7	Timed Drill 8	Warm-up 5	Timed Drill 9	Warm-up 6	Timed Drill 10	Timed Drill 11	Review A	Review B	Review C
GOAL 1: Problem Solving	• build new mathematical knowledge through problem solving;	✓	✓	✓	✓	✓	✓	✓	✓	✓	✓	✓	✓	✓	✓	✓	✓	✓	✓	✓	✓
	• solve problems that arise in mathematics and in other contexts;	✓	✓	✓	✓	✓	✓	✓	✓	✓	✓	✓	✓	✓	✓	✓	✓	✓	✓	✓	✓
	• apply and adapt a variety of appropriate strategies to solve problems;		✓				✓	✓	✓		✓	✓	✓	✓		✓	✓	✓	✓	✓	✓
	• monitor and reflect on the process of mathematical problem solving.		✓	✓	✓	✓	✓	✓	✓	✓	✓	✓	✓	✓		✓	✓	✓	✓	✓	✓
GOAL 2: Reasoning & Proof	• recognize reasoning and proof as fundamental aspects of mathematics;			✓		✓		✓	✓	✓	✓	✓	✓	✓		✓	✓	✓	✓	✓	✓
	• make and investigate mathematical conjectures;	✓	✓	✓	✓	✓	✓	✓	✓	✓	✓	✓	✓	✓	✓	✓	✓	✓	✓	✓	✓
	• develop and evaluate mathematical arguments and proofs;	✓	✓	✓		✓	✓	✓	✓	✓	✓	✓	✓	✓		✓	✓	✓	✓	✓	✓
	• select and use various types of reasoning and methods of proof.																				
GOAL 3: Communication	• organize and consolidate their mathematical thinking through communication;	✓	✓	✓	✓	✓	✓	✓	✓	✓	✓	✓	✓	✓	✓	✓	✓	✓	✓	✓	✓
	• communicate their mathematical thinking coherently and clearly to peers, teachers, and others;	✓	✓	✓	✓	✓	✓	✓	✓	✓	✓	✓	✓	✓	✓	✓	✓	✓	✓	✓	✓
	• analyze and evaluate the mathematical thinking and strategies of others;	✓	✓	✓		✓			✓	✓	✓	✓	✓	✓	✓	✓	✓	✓	✓	✓	✓
	• use the language of mathematics to express mathematical ideas precisely.	✓	✓	✓	✓	✓	✓	✓	✓	✓	✓	✓	✓	✓	✓	✓	✓	✓	✓	✓	✓
GOAL 4: Connections	• recognize and use connections among mathematical ideas;	✓	✓		✓		✓	✓	✓			✓	✓	✓		✓	✓	✓	✓	✓	
	• understand how mathematical ideas interconnect and build on one another to produce a coherent whole;	✓		✓	✓	✓	✓	✓	✓			✓	✓	✓			✓	✓	✓	✓	
	• recognize and apply mathematics in contexts outside of mathematics.	✓	✓	✓	✓		✓	✓		✓		✓		✓		✓	✓		✓	✓	
GOAL 5: Representation	• create and use representations to organize, record, and communicate mathematical ideas;	✓	✓	✓	✓	✓	✓	✓	✓	✓	✓	✓	✓	✓	✓	✓	✓	✓	✓	✓	✓
	• select, apply, and translate among mathematical representations to solve problems;	✓	✓	✓	✓	✓	✓	✓	✓	✓	✓	✓	✓	✓	✓	✓	✓	✓	✓	✓	✓
	• use representations to model and interpret physical, social, and mathematical phenomena.	✓	✓	✓	✓	✓	✓	✓	✓	✓	✓	✓	✓	✓	✓	✓	✓	✓	✓	✓	✓

Contents

TEACHER GUIDE

STUDENT HANDOUTS

Algebra – Task Sheets

✔ **6 BONUS Activity Pages! Additional worksheets for your students**

- Go to our website: **www.classroomcompletepress.com/bonus**
- Enter item CC3107
- Enter pass code CC3107D for Activity Pages.

Contents

STUDENT HANDOUTS

NCTM Content Standards Assessment Rubric

Algebra – Task & Drill Sheets

Student's Name: ______________ Assignment: ______________ Level: ______________

	Level 1	Level 2	Level 3	Level 4
Understanding Sorting, Patterning, Graphing, Equations and Quantitative Change	• Demonstrates a limited understanding of Sorting, Patterning, Graphing, Equations and Quantitative Change	• Demonstrates a basic understanding of Sorting, Patterning, Graphing, Equations and Quantitative Change	• Demonstrates a good understanding of Sorting, Patterning, Graphing, Equations and Quantitative Change	• Demonstrates a thorough understanding of Sorting, Patterning, Graphing, Equations and Quantitative Change
Applying Appropriate Technique, Tools, and Formulas to Solve Algebraic Problems	• Demonstrates limited ability in using formulas to solve algebraic equations	• Demonstrates some ability in using formulas to solve algebraic equations	• Demonstrates satisfactory ability in using formulas to solve algebraic equations	• Demonstrates strong ability in using formulas to solve algebraic equations

STRENGTHS:

WEAKNESSES:

NEXT STEPS:

Teacher Guide

Our resource has been created for ease of use by both TEACHERS and STUDENTS alike.

Introduction

The NCTM content standards have been used in the creation of the assignments in this booklet. This method promotes the idea that it is beneficial to learn through practical, applicable, real-world examples. Many of the task and drill sheets are organized around a central problem taken from real-life experiences of the students. The pages of this booklet contain a variety in terms of levels of difficulty and content so as to provide students with a variety of different opportunities. Included are opportunities for problem-solving, sorting, patterning, algebraic graphing, solving equations, examining quantitative change, evaluating algebraic expressions, utilizing number lines and graphs, mathematical sentences and algebraic properties. Visual models are included to assist visual learners. Teachers may also choose to use mathematics manipulatives along with the exercises included in this book to help address the needs of kinesthetic learners.

How Is Our Resource Organized?

STUDENT HANDOUTS

Reproducible **task sheets** and **drill sheets** make up the majority of our resource.

The **task sheets** contain challenging problem-solving tasks in drill form, many centered around 'real-world' ideas or problems, which push the boundaries of critical thought and demonstrate to students why mathematics is important and applicable in the real world. It is not expected that all activities will be used, but are offered for variety and flexibility in teaching and assessment. Many of the drill sheet problems offer space for reflection, and opportunity for the appropriate use of technology, as encouraged by the NCTM's *Principles & Standards for School Mathematics*.

The **drill sheets** contain 11 Timed Drill Sheets and 6 Warm-Up Drill Sheets, featuring real-life problem-solving opportunities. The drill sheets are provided to help students with their procedural proficiency skills, as emphasized by the *NCTM's Curriculum Focal Points*.

The **NCTM Content Standards Assessment Rubric** (*page 6*) is a useful tool for evaluating students' work in many of the activities in our resource. The **Reviews** (*pages 26-28* and *46-48*) are divided by grade and can be used for a follow-up review or assessment at the completion of the unit.

PICTURE CUES

Our resource contains three main types of pages, each with a different purpose and use. A **Picture Cue** at the top of each page shows, at a glance, what the page is for.

Teacher Guide

* Information and tools for the teacher

Student Handout

* Reproducible drill sheets

Easy Marking™ Answer Key

* Answers for student activities

Timed Drill Stopwatch

* Write the amount of time for students to complete the timed drill sheet in the stopwatch. Recommended times are given on the contents page.

EASY MARKING™ ANSWER KEY

Marking students' worksheets is fast and easy with our **Answer Key**. Answers are listed in columns – just line up the column with its corresponding worksheet, as shown, and see how every question matches up with its answer!

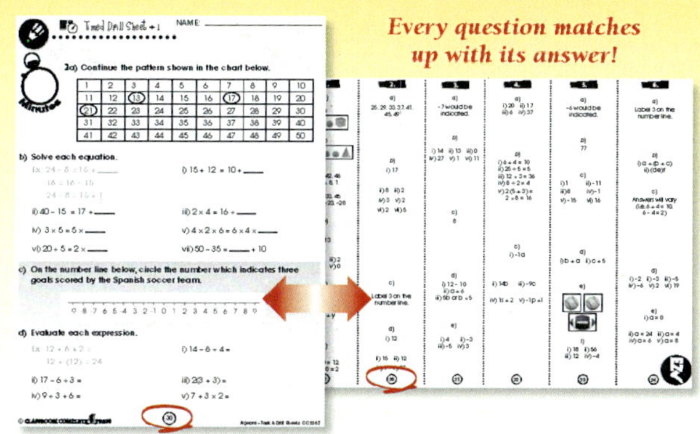

Principles & Standards

***Principles & Standards for School Mathematics* outlines the essential components of an effective school mathematics program.**

The NCTM's Principles & Standards for School Mathematics

The **Principles** are the fundamentals to an effective mathematics education. The **Standards** are descriptions of what mathematics instruction should enable students to learn. Together the **Principles and Standards** offer a comprehensive and coherent set of learning goals, serving as a resource to teachers and a framework for curriculum. Our resource offers exercises written to the NCTM **Process** and **Content Standards** and is inspired by the **Principles** outlined below.

Six Principles for School Mathematics

Equity

EQUITY: All students can learn mathematics when they have access to high-quality instruction, including reasonable and appropriate accommodation and appropriately challenging content.

Curriculum

CURRICULUM: The curriculum must be coherent, focused, and well articulated across the grades, with ideas linked to and building on one another to deepen students' knowledge and understanding.

Teaching

TEACHING: Effective teaching requires understanding what students know and need to learn and then challenging and supporting them to learn it well.

Learning

LEARNING: By aligning factual knowledge and procedural proficiency with conceptual knowledge, students can become effective learners, reflecting on their thinking and learning from their mistakes.

Assessment

ASSESSMENT: The tasks teachers select for assessment convey a message to students about what kinds of knowledge and performance are valued. Feedback promotes goal-setting, responsibility, and independence.

Technology

TECHNOLOGY: Students can develop a deeper understanding of mathematics with the appropriate use of technology, which can allow them to focus on decision-making, reflection, reasoning, and problem solving.

Our resource correlates to the six Principles and provides teachers with supplementary materials, which can aid them in fulfilling the expectations of each principle. The exercises provided allow for variety and flexibility in teaching and assessment. The topical division of concepts and processes promotes linkage and the building of conceptual knowledge and understanding throughout the student's grade and elementary school career. Each of the drill sheet problems help students with their procedural proficiency skills, and offers space for reflection and opportunity for the appropriate use of technology.

Task Sheet 1

1) **Kerri moves to a new neighborhood. She finds two video stores within walking distance of her home. She finds that the two stores offer very different rental plans for their DVDs.**

Jon-Mark's Video Palace: Charges an annual membership fee of $25. Each rental is $2.

a) **Use the following equation to calculate the cost to Kerri for a year's membership if she rents a total of 25 videos.**
$C = 25 + 2x$

____

____

____

Nothin' But the Hits Rental: Does not charge a membership fee, but the rental for each DVD is $2.75

b) **Use the following equation to calculate the cost to Kerri for a year if she rents a total of 25 videos.** $C = 2.75x$

____

____

____

c) **Which would be the better deal? By how much?**

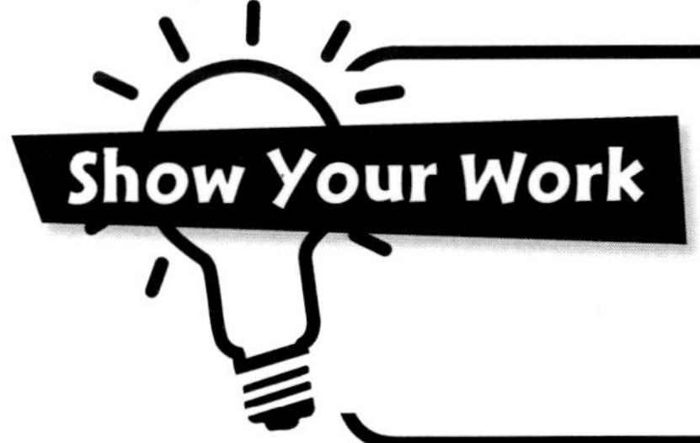

Answer: ______________________

NAME: ______________________

Task Sheet 2

2) Using the equations given in Task Sheet 1, which would be the better deal for Kerry (and by how much) if she rented 50 movies in a given year?

a) Jon-Mark's Video Palace: ______________

b) Nothin' But the Hits Rental:: ______________

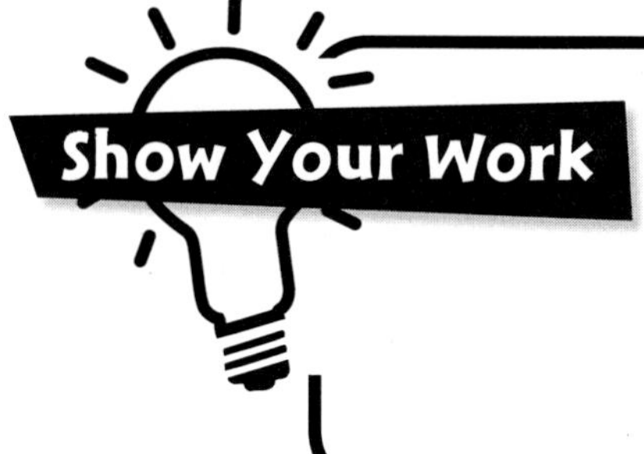

c) Best Deal Answer: ______________

d) Given the above results, what factor would be important when deciding which would be the better deal?

____

e) What is the value of x in the following: (Show your work.)

i) x + 7 = 12 — x: ______

ii) 13 – x = 6 — x: ______

iii) 7x = 42 — x: ______

iv) x / 9 = 7 — x: ______

Explore With Technology

Use a calculator to answer the following:

Write down the number of the month in which you were born. Multiply this number by 10. Add 20 to this result. Multiply the answer by 10 then add 165. Now add your present age to the result. Subtract 365. The result should be the number of your birth month, followed by your current age!

NAME: ______________________________

Task Sheet 3

3) Graph each solution on the accompanying number line.

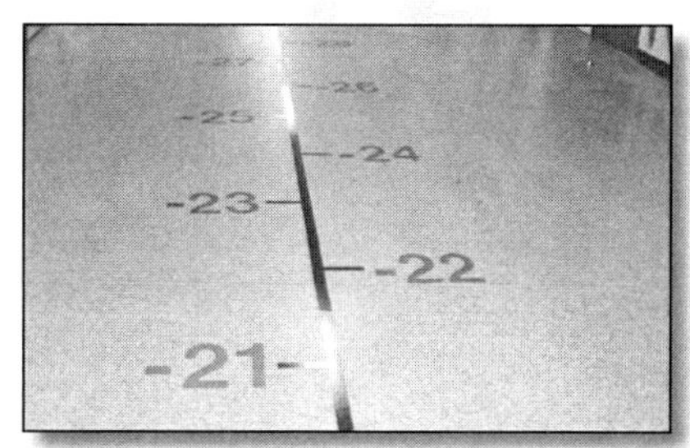

a) $x = -4$

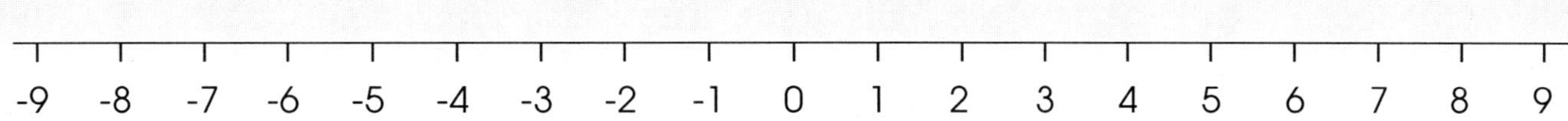

b) $x < 1$

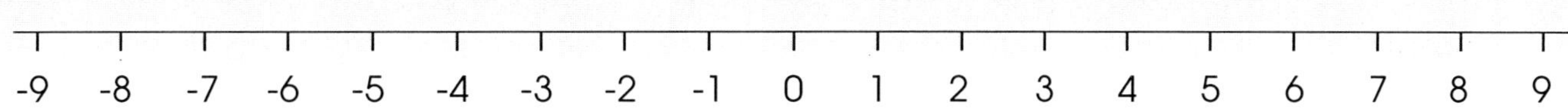

c) $x = 2$ **and** $y = -7$

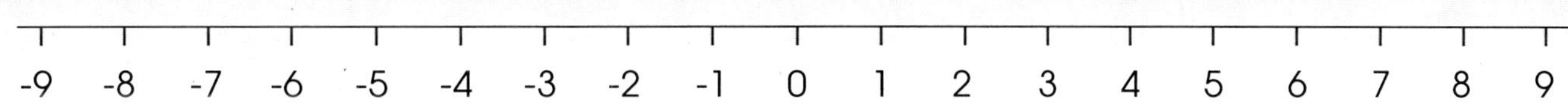

d) $x \geq -6$

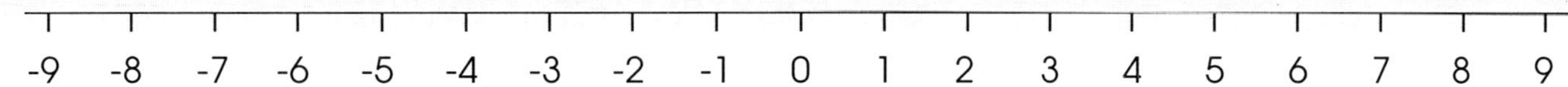

e) **On the graph below, indicate the solution to x.**

$x + 2 = 6$

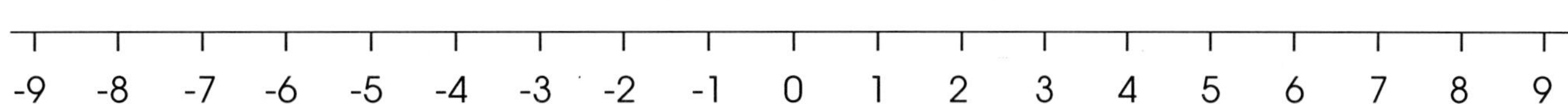

1 + 2 Task Sheet

NAME: ______________________

Task Sheet 4

4a) What is the missing term in the decreasing pattern below?

302, 287, 272, ______, 242

b) A pattern is shown below. Each term increases by the same amount.

17, 26, 35, 44 ...

What is the eighth term in this pattern? Answer: ______________

c) The following pattern increases by the following rule: multiply the previous term by 3 and add 2.

7, 23, 71, 215 ...

What is the next term in the sequence?

i) 647 ii) 432 iii) 612 iv) 587

Explain the rule describing each of the following sequence of numbers:

d) 3, 5, 7, 9, 11 . . .

____

____

e) 3, 6, 9, 12, 15 . . .

____

____

f) 1, 4, 9, 16, 25 . . .

____

____

NAME: ____________________

Task Sheet 5

5a) Caleb can buy a bag of chips for .75¢ and a soda for .80¢. If Caleb can buy **B** bags of chips at .75¢ each and **S** sodas at .80¢ each, what is the meaning of: *(Show your work!)*

a) **B + S**

Answer: ____________

b) **15B**

Answer: ____________

c) **12S**

Answer: ____________

d) **14B + 8S**

Answer: ____________

Explore With Technology

Visit the Math website http://www.aplusmath.com/.

As well as an Algebra section, the site also includes a Game Room, Flash Cards, Homework Helper, and Worksheets.

Algebra Planet Blaster – is a fun interactive game where students can practice their skills. Try it!

NAME: ______________________

Task Sheet 6

6a) From the following graph, give the coordinates for the four objects indicated.

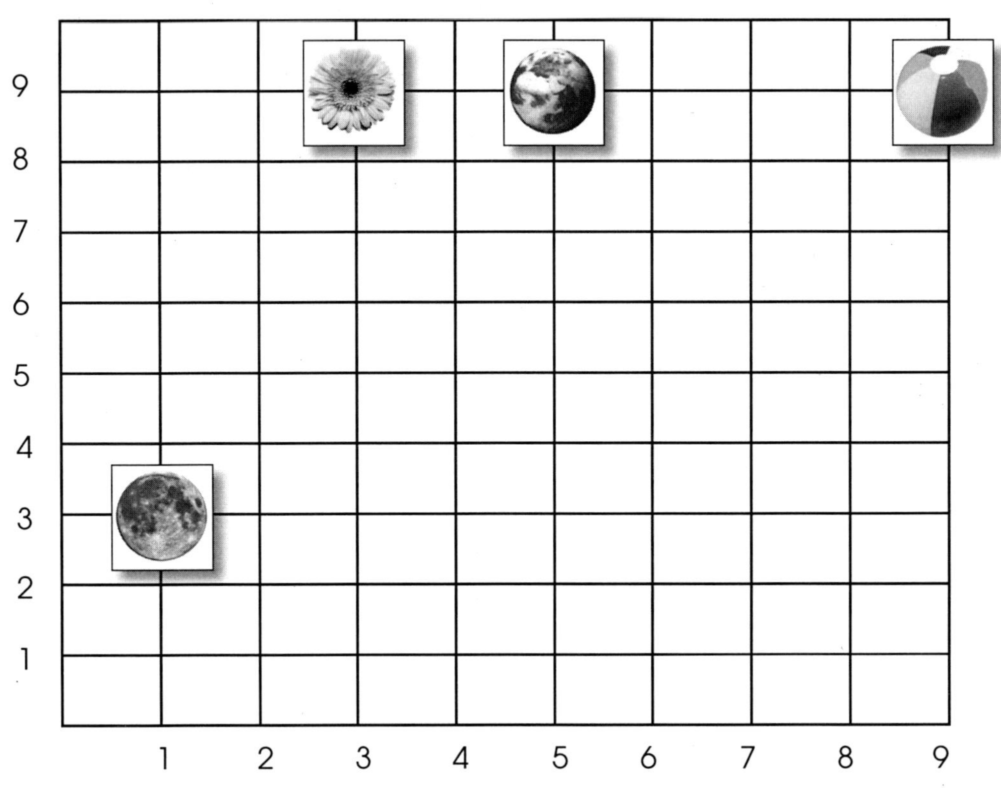

Coordinates

 ______________________

 ______________________

 ______________________

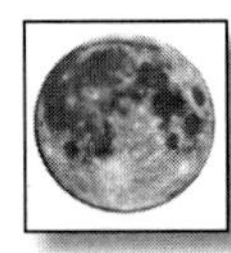 ______________________

NAME: ______________________________

Task Sheet 7

7) Solve the following equations. Show your work.

a) $7 + x = 15$

b) $9 - 2 = x + 1$

c) $2x = 14 - 2$

d) The Wrong Step! Mike shows his steps when solving the following equation for x:

$2x + 1 = 19$

Step 1: $2x + 1 - 1 = 19 - 1$

Step 2: $2x = 18$

Step 3: $x = 18 \times 2$

Step 4: $x = 36$

In which step did Mike make an error?

i) Step 1   ii) Step 2   iii) Step 3   iv) Step 4

Answer: ____________________

e) If $y = 6$, what is the value of $24 - (3 \times y)$?

i) 8   ii) 6   iii) 10   iv) 4

NAME: ______________________

Task Sheet 8

8a) Examine the input-output table shown below.

Input	Output
4	11
5	13
6	15
8	19

Which of these rules describes the data?

i) Add 1 and multiply by 2.

ii) Add 8 then subtract 1.

iii) Multiply by 2 and add 4.

iv) Multiply by 2 and add 3.

b) Examine the input-output table shown below.

Input	Output
12	8
16	10
22	13
8	6

Which of these rules describes the data?

i) Subtract by 4 then multiply by 1.

ii) Multiply by 2 and add 2.

iii) Divide by 2 and add 2.

iv) Divide by 3 then add 4.

c) This month Jose's hockey team played four games. During these games, the team scored 7, 2, 3 and 0 goals. What was the average number of goals per game that the team scored?

Answer: ______________

NAME: ______________________________

Task Sheet 9

9) For the final fundraiser at Randy's school, they decide to hold a soap box derby. Several races will be held at The Old Fair Grounds. General Admission to The Old Fair Grounds is \$5. Admission to <u>each</u> race is an extra \$2. The algebraic expression to represent this is $C = 5x + 2x$.

a) If 250 people came to the races, how much money would be collected by the Admissions?

b) As a part of their expenses for the day, the school had to rent the Old Fair Grounds from the city for \$100. Deduct this from the Admissions Profits in a).

c) In addition to the profits the school made from the Admissions to the events, they also sold food and drinks. Drinks were priced at \$1.25; hot dogs at \$2; hamburgers at \$2.50 and cotton candy at \$3. All the food and drinks were donated by local companies so the money raised was profit. Complete the following chart showing how much was raised. Then give the chart a <u>total</u>.

	Cost	# Sold	Profit
Drinks	1.25	200	
Hot Dogs	2.00	175	
Hamburgers	2.50	120	
Cotton Candy	3.00	302	
TOTAL PROFIT			

1+2 Task Sheet

NAME: ____________________

Task Sheet 10

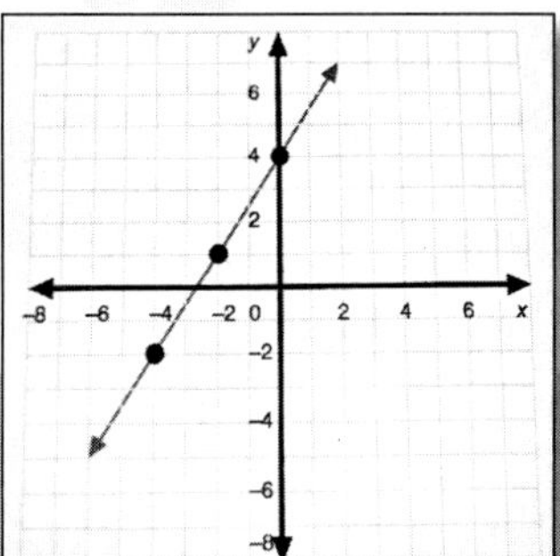

10) Plot the following coordinates on the accompanying grid:

a) **A = (2, 5)**

B = (6, -5)

C = (-4, 8)

D = (-6, -6)

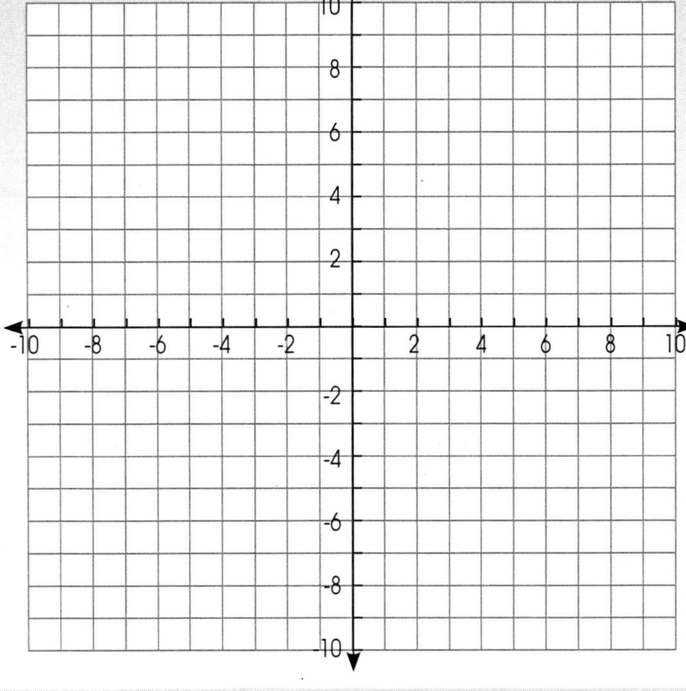

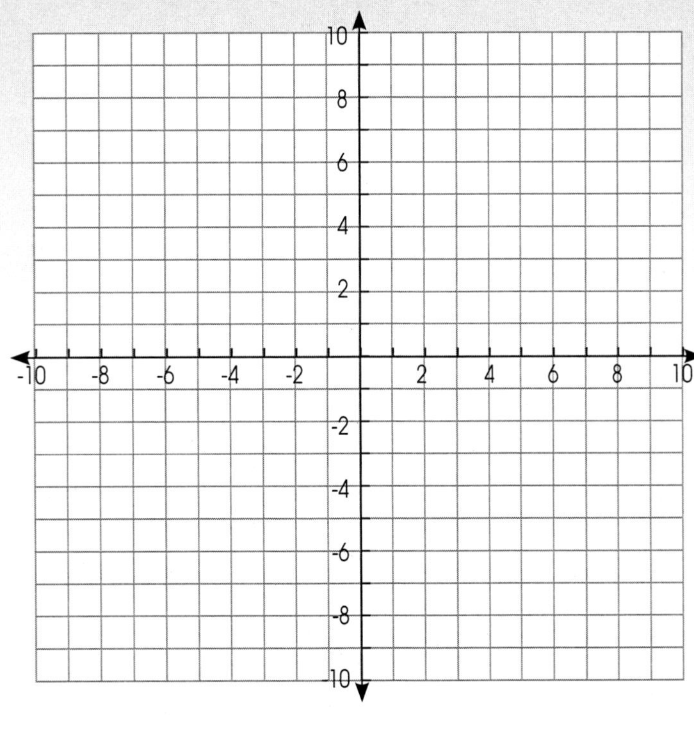

b) **E = (3, 10)**

F = (8, -3)

G = (-5, 0)

H = (-10, -1)

Task Sheet 11

11) Sara's mom sends her down to the mall to pick up chicken dinner for the family. Sara visits two stores in the mall which sell chicken. Both stores sell chicken by the bucket, but Sara's family is quite large, so they will need more than one bucket for dinner. Here is a comparison of prices:

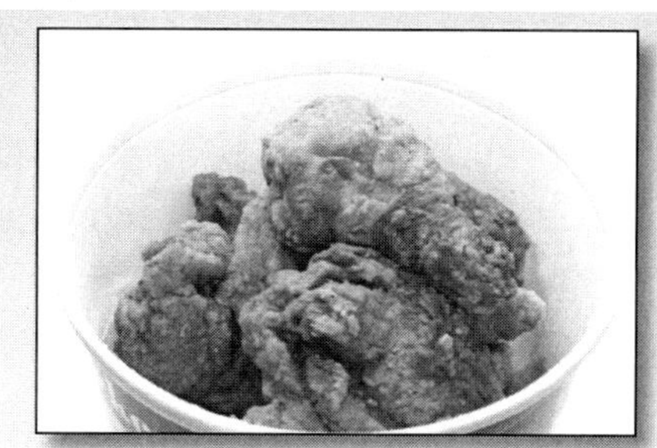

Store A	\$15.00 / bucket **(b)**	\$2.00 / piece **(p)**
Store B	\$17.50 / bucket **(b)**	\$1.00 / piece **(p)**

Sara decides to apply her knowledge of algebra to solve the problem of which store offers the best price. In the chart below are the formulas that Sara will use. Solve these problems for her. The letter **C** will represent the total cost, the letter **b** will represent the bucket of chicken, and the letter **p** will represent the extra pieces of chicken she needs to buy. The letter **x** will represent the number of extra pieces that Sara will need to buy.

Store A	$C = b + xp$	5 extra pieces	Total cost:
Store B	$C = b + xp$	5 extra pieces	Total cost:

Show Your Work

Store A:

Answer: ______________

Store B:

Answer: ______________

Which Store offers the better deal for Sara? ______________

By how much? ______________

Jessica joined the local bowling league this winter. Her best four games for one week were 142, 128, 214 and 132. **Use a calculator to determine her average score for the week.**

NAME: ____________________

Task Sheet

Task Sheet 12

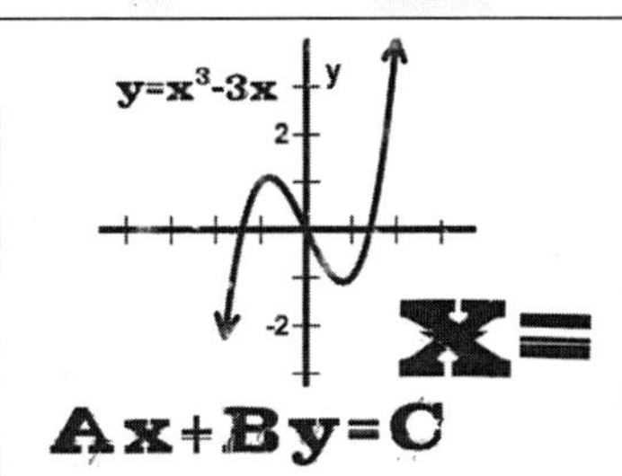

12a) If x = 2 and y = 3, which expression has the largest value?

i) xy ii) x + y iii) y – x

Show Your Work

xy: **x + y:** **y - x:**

b) Order is very important in completing algebraic problems. For instance:

- **Always do what's in the brackets first**
- **Multiplying and dividing come before adding and subtracting**

Solve the problems below.

i) 2 x 3 + 2 = ii) 4 x 2 – 7 =

iii) 7 x 3 – 8 = iv) 14 / 2 + 6 =

c) Solve the following questions if x = 4.

i) x – 7 = ☐ ii) 2 + ☐ = x

d) Solve the following question if y = 9.

i) y / 3 = ☐ ii) y + 3 + 6 – 2 = ☐

e) Solve the following questions if n = 5.

i) n x 7 = ☐ ii) 55 / n = ☐ iii) 74 – n = ☐

NAME: ____________________________________

Task Sheet 13

13.  = x and = 1

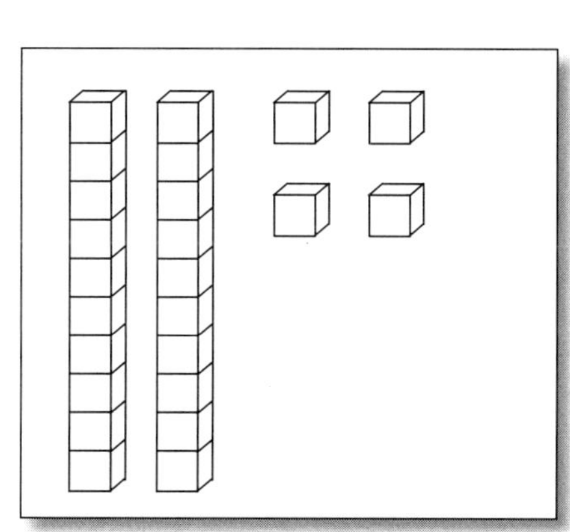

=

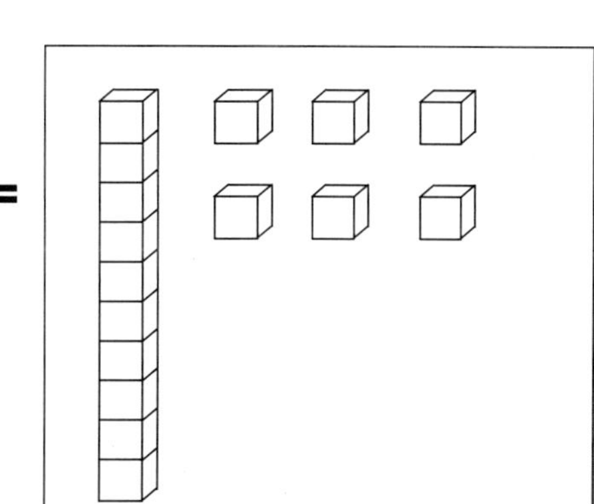

This can be represented as $2x + 4 = x + 6$

a) Remove the same number of tiles from each side, making sure that you keep both sides in balance. What do you have left?

i) $2x = 1$ ii) $x = 2$ iii) $4 + x = 2x$ iv) $2 + 2x = 0$

b) How might the following be written as an equation?

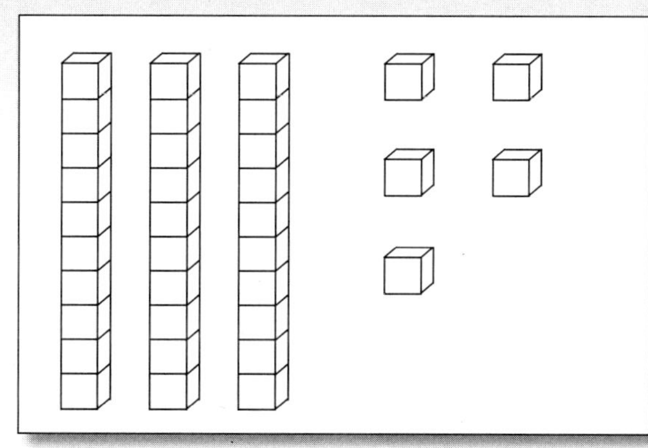

=

i) $3x + 7 = 2x + 7$ ii) $2x + 7 = 3x + 4$ iii) $3x + 4 = 2x - 7$ iv) $3x + 5 = 2x + 7$

NAME: ______________________

Task Sheet 14

14.

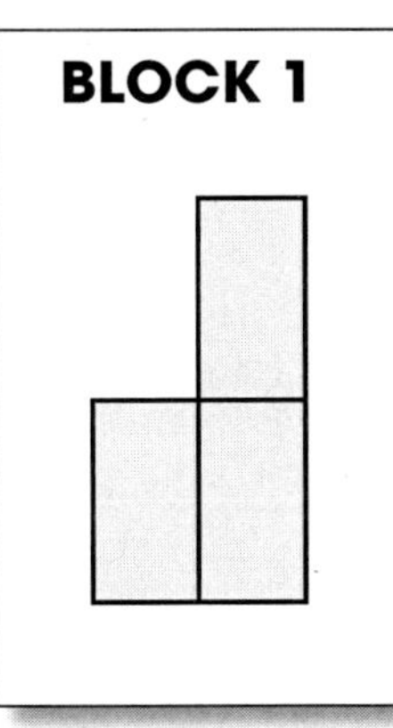

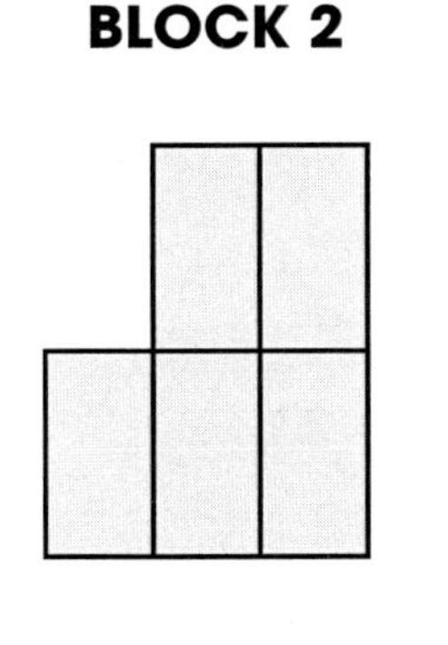

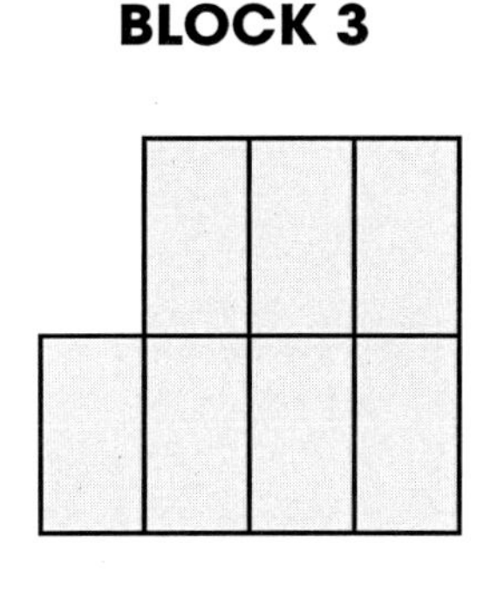

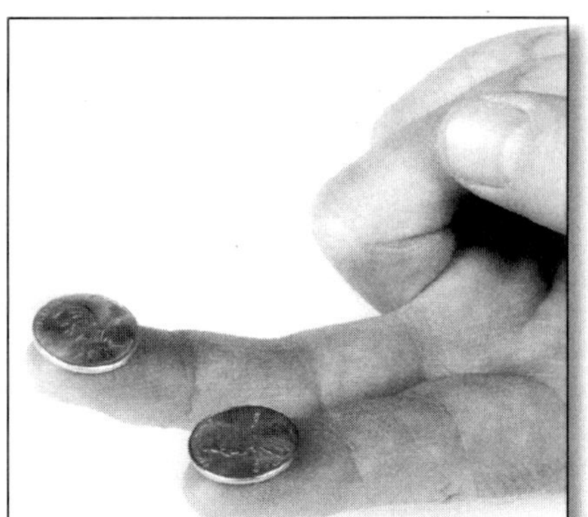

a) If the pattern in Blocks 1, 2, and 3 continue, how many rectangles would it take to make the 5th Block?

Answer: ______________

b) How many rectangles would it take to make the 10th Block?

Answer: ______________

c) I have .42¢ in my pocket. I have only dimes and pennies. What coins might I have? Complete the chart below showing the possibilities.

Dimes	Pennies	Total

The website http://www.coolmath.com, has a very helpful Algebra section. It has a lot of great tutorials and fun activities – even a graphing calculator that students can experiment with. Play around on the site, and try your hand at some algebraic problems.

NAME: ______________________________

Task Sheet 15

15a) This table shows how much it costs to rent a DVD from *Paul's Movies and Games*. **Choose which equation matches the table.**

Days Rented **(x)**	0	1	2	3	4
Cost to Rent **(C)**	4	6	8	10	12

i) $C = 2x + 4$ ii) $C = x + 2$ iii) $C = 0x + 2$ iv) $C = x + 4$

b) Maria rented a movie from Paul's Movies and Games. Her bill came to $8. Plot this amount on the line below.

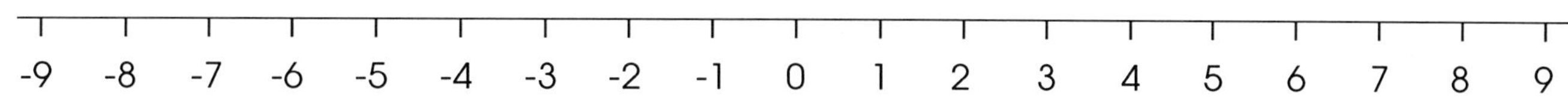

c) Solve the following equations:

i) $x + 17 = 72$ ii) $x - 43 = 12$ iii) $99 - x = 40$

d) What is the solution to this equation?
$4x - 6 = 2x + 30$

i) $x = 14$ ii) $x = 12$ iii) $x = 18$ iv) $x = 32$

Explore With Technology

Order of operations is very important when performing a mathematical calculation. Remember that in an equation, multiplication and division are performed before addition and subtraction. Using a calculator, perform the underlined parts in the following two equations first — then record your answers to both. What a difference this can make!!

- $\underline{3 + 5} \times 2 =$
- $3 + \underline{5 \times 2} =$
- $\underline{7 - 2} \times 3 =$
- $7 - \underline{2 \times 3} =$

NAME: ______________________

Drill Sheet 1

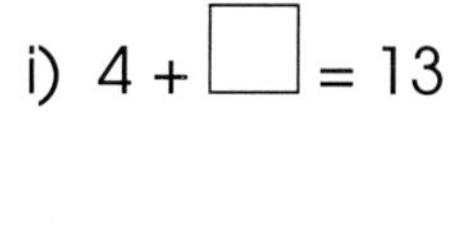

a) Determine the value of $\square$ in the following equations. Show your work.

i) $4 + \square = 13$

ii) $17 - \square = 9$

iii) $9 \times \square = 63$

iv) $\square \div 7 = 8$

b) Graph on the accompanying number line.

x = 7

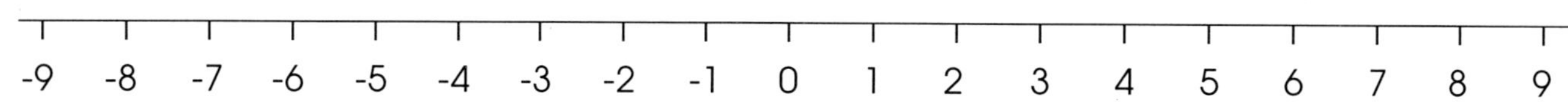

c) What is the missing term in the increasing pattern below?

199, 213, 227, ____, 255

d) Solve showing your work:

i) $3x - 2 = 7$

ii) $7x + 3 = 27 - 3$

iii) $4x = 32$

iv) $4x = 7 + 3 \times 3$

v) $x \div 4 = 24$

vi) $4 + 16 \div 4 = x$

NAME: ____________________

Drill Sheet 2

a) **A pattern is shown below. Each term decreases by the same amount.**

80, 71, 62, 53 ...

What is the seventh term in this pattern?

Answer:____________

b) **Solve the following equations if x = 6. Show your work.**

i) $x + 4 =$ ii) $9 - x + 2x =$ iii) $4x - (5 \times 5 - 17) =$

c) **What is the average of the following marks out of 100?**

76, 82, 91, 66, 100

Show your work.

Answer:____________

d) **Graph on the accompanying number line.**

$-2 < x < 4$

-9 -8 -7 -6 -5 -4 -3 -2 -1 0 1 2 3 4 5 6 7 8 9

Review A

a) Determine the value of ☐ in the following equations. Show your work.

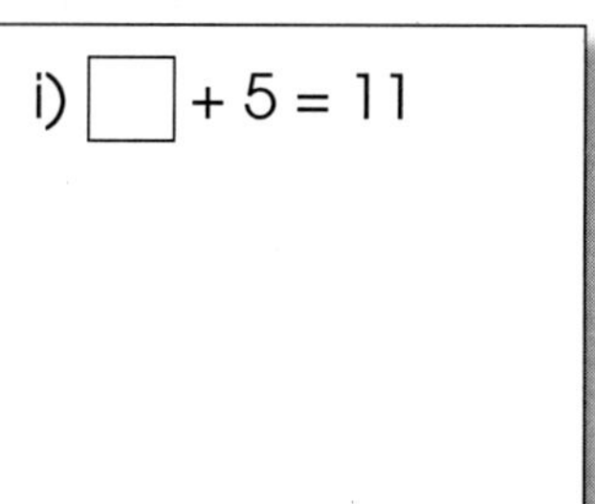

i) ☐ + 5 = 11

ii) 12 - ☐ = 6

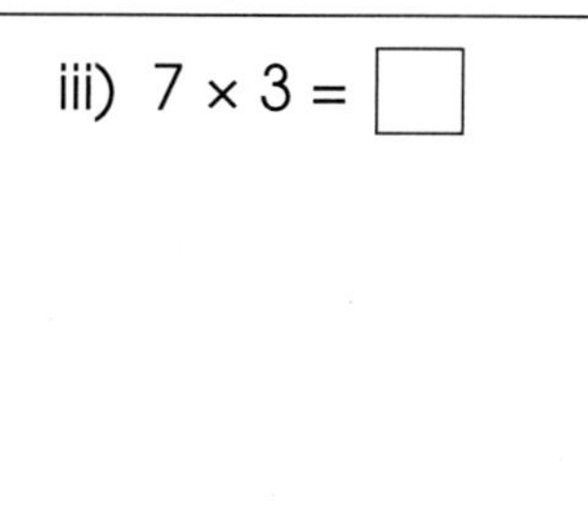

iii) 7 × 3 = ☐

iv) 10 - ☐ = 3 × 2

b) Graph on the accompanying number line.

x = 9

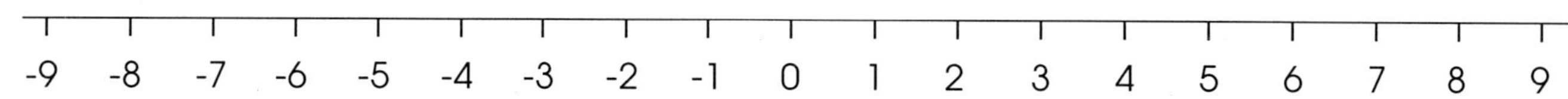

c) What is the missing term in the increasing pattern below?

24, 26, ___, 30, 32 . . .

d) 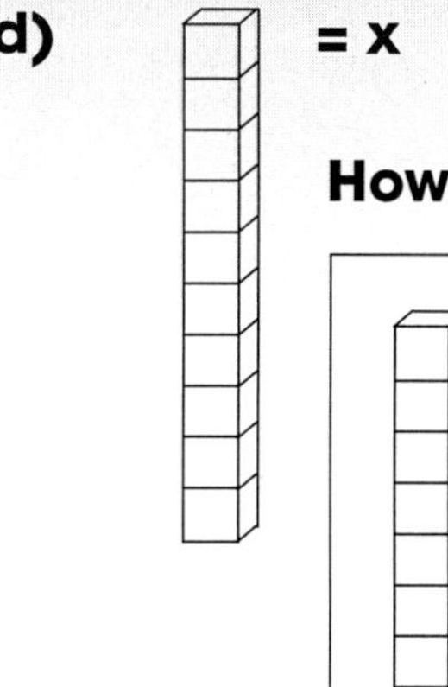 **= x and**  **= 1.**

How might the following be written as an equation?

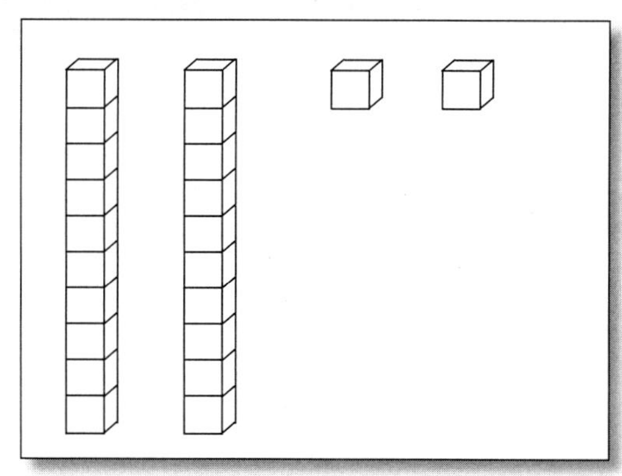

=

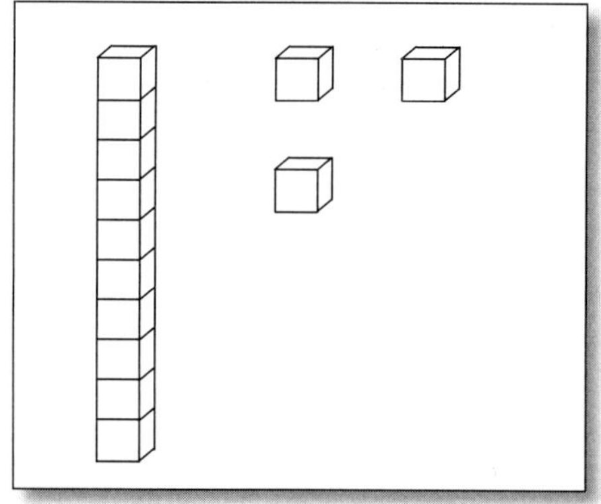

i) 2x – 2 = 1 x + 2 ii) 3x + 1 = 2x + 3 iii) 2x + 2 = 1x + 3 iv) 2x + 2 = 3x + 3

NAME: ______________________________

Review B

a) Solve the following equations:

i) $21 - x = 12$

ii) $x \times 7 = 56$

iii) $x \div 12 = 5$

b) If x = 8, solve these equations.

i) $2x - 7 =$

ii) $4 \times x =$

iii) $3x + 1 =$

c) Graph on the accompanying number line. $-8 < x < 9$

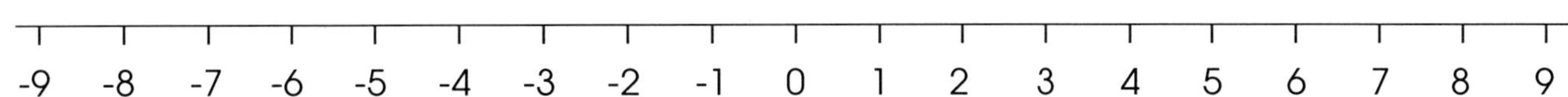

d) Jason's dad rents a table saw to help build a dog house for Rover. This table shows how much it costs to rent the table saw from Moe's Rentals. Choose which equation matches the table.

Days Rented **(x)**	0	1	2	3	4
Cost to Rent **(C)**	10	15	20	25	30

i) $C = 5x + 10$ ii) $C = 10x + 5$ iii) $C = x + 15$ iv) $C = 15x + 10$

e) Find the average for Julia's bowling scores: 156, 116, 212, 96

Answer: ______________________

NAME: ______________________________

Review C

a) Solve the following equations:

i) $4x + 3 = 2x + 7$

ii) $7x - 3 = 5x + 9$

iii) $-7 + 6x = 4 - 3 + 4x - 2x$

b) If x = 7, solve these equations.

i) $6x + 3x + 4 =$

ii) $2x^2 + 8x + 17 - 12 =$

iii) $x^2 + 3x =$

c) Graph on the accompanying number line: $-5 \leq x \leq 4$

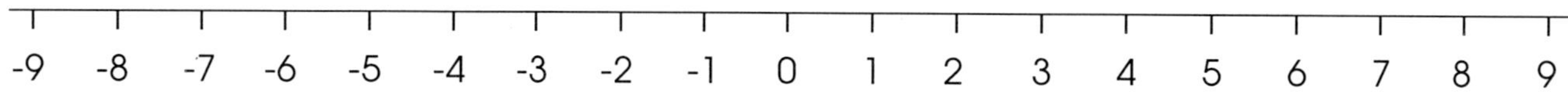

d) Jessica and her family decide to rent a wave runner for their vacation at the cottage. The local marina charges a flat fee of \$50 (f) plus \$25 per day (x). Use the following equation to determine how much Jessica's family would pay to rent the wave runner for 5 days. $C = f + 25x$

Answer: ______________________

e) Find the average of the amount of money Joey earns on his paper route over a five day period.

\$6.70, \$7.50, \$12.30, \$10.00, \$8.80

Answer: ______________________

NAME: ______________________________

Warm-Up Drill Sheet # 1

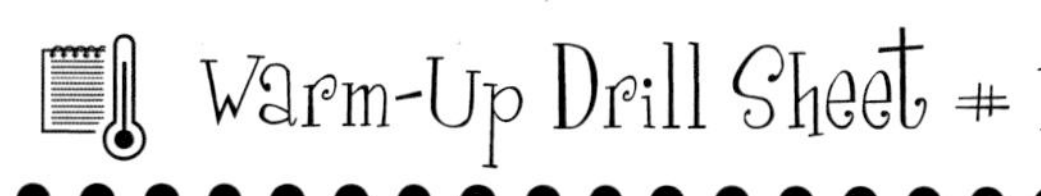

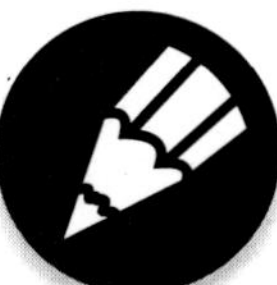

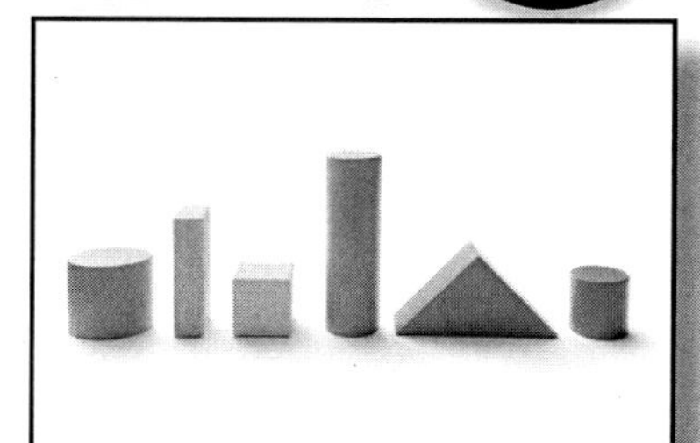

1a) Complete the following patterns.

i) _____ _____ _____ _____

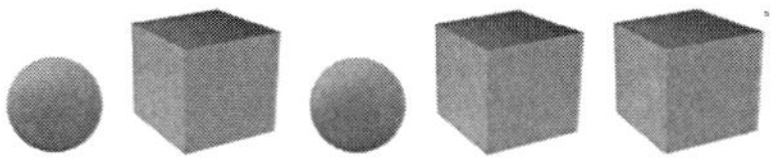

ii) _____ _____ _____ _____ _____

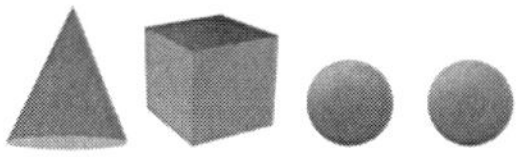

iii) 26, 30, 34, _____, _____, _____

iv) 36, 29, 22, _____, _____, _____

v) 15, _____, 27, _____, 39, _____

vi) –3, –8, –13, _____, _____, _____

b) Evaluate each expression

Ex: Let a = 3 **12 + a =**
12 + 3 = 15

i) Let b = 4 17 – b =

ii) Let c = 7 7 × c =

iii) Let d = 5 9 – d – 2 =

iv) Let e = 2 –8 ÷ e =

v) Let f = 0 14 × f =

c) Rewrite the following using the commutative property.

Ex: **x + 5 = 5 + x**

i) a + b ______________________

ii) y + 3 ______________________

d) Determine the missing members of the following number family.

10 + 2 = 12

12 – 2 = 10

____

____

Timed Drill Sheet # 1

NAME: ____________________

2a) Continue the pattern shown in the chart below.

1	2	3	4	5	6	7	8	9	10
11	12	(13)	14	15	16	(17)	18	19	20
(21)	22	23	24	25	26	27	28	29	30
31	32	33	34	35	36	37	38	39	40
41	42	43	44	45	46	47	48	49	50

b) Solve each equation.

Ex: 24 – 8 = 15 + ____

16 = 16 – 15

24 – 8 = 15 + 1

i) 15 + 12 = 10 + ____

ii) 40 – 15 = 17 + ____

iii) 2 × 4 = 16 ÷ ____

iv) 3 × 5 = 5 × ____

v) 4 × 2 × 6 = 6 × 4 × ____

vi) 20 ÷ 5 = 2 × ____

vii) 50 – 35 = ____ + 10

c) On the number line below, circle the number which indicates three goals scored by the Spanish soccer team.

-9 -8 -7 -6 -5 -4 -3 -2 -1 0 1 2 3 4 5 6 7 8 9

d) Evaluate each expression.

Ex: 12 + 6 × 2 =

12 + (12) = 24

i) 14 – 8 ÷ 4 =

ii) 17 – 6 ÷ 3 =

iii) 2(3 + 3) =

iv) 9 ÷ 3 + 6 =

v) 7 + 3 × 2 =

NAME: ______________________

3a) On the number line below, circle the number which indicates seven steps backward.

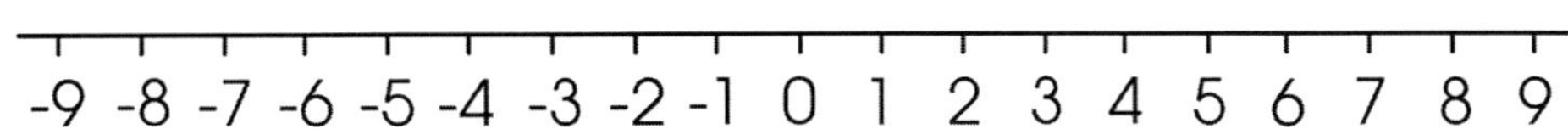

b) Solve the following.

i) 14 + 0 = _____ ii) 13 × 1 = _____ iii) 42 × 0 = _____

iv) 17 + 10 = _____ v) 12 ÷ 12 = _____ vi) 88 – 77 = _____

c) Consider the following pattern.

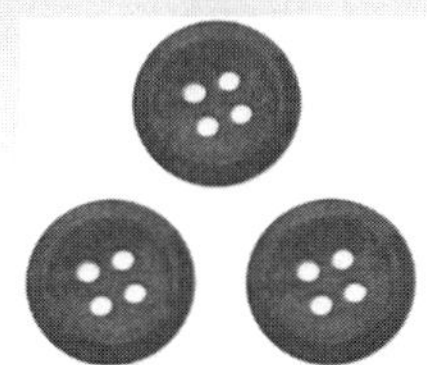
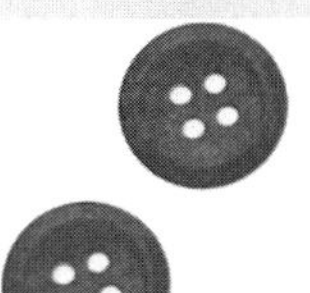
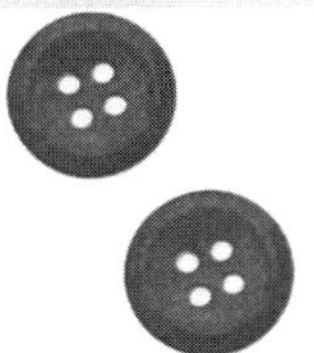

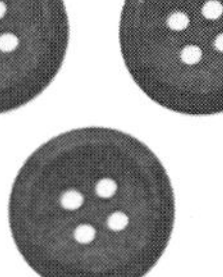

If the pattern continues in the same way, how many circles will be in the <u>sixth</u> term? Answer: __________

d) Write each of the following as an algebraic expression.

Ex: The sum of 2 and 6. <u>2 + 6</u>

i) The difference of 12 and 10. ______________________

ii) ***a*** increased by 6. ______________________

iii) The product of ***b*** and 5. ______________________

e) Find each quotient. **Ex: 6 ÷ 2 = 3**

i) 12 ÷ 3 = ii) –18 ÷ 6 =

iii) 15 ÷ –3 = iv) 9 ÷ 3 =

Warm-Up Drill Sheet # 2 NAME: ____________________

4a) Evaluate each expression.

Ex: 2(2 + 3) = 2(5) = 2 × 5 = 10

i) $2(4 + 6) =$

ii) $5 + 2 \times 6 =$

iii) $36 \div (4 + 2) =$

iv) $20 + 16 - 9 + 10 =$

b) Evaluate these expressions.

Ex: 6 – a, where a = 2

6 – 2 = 4

i) $a + 4$, where $a = 6$

ii) $25 \div b$, where $b = 5$

iii) $12c$, where $c = 3$

iv) $a \div b$, where $a = 8$ and $b = 2$

v) $2(c + d)$, where $c = 5$ and $d = 3$

c) Simplify the following expressions.

Ex: –4z + 5z =

–4 + 5 = 1z

i) $-2a + 3a - 2a =$

ii) $17b - 3b =$

iii) $-5c - 3c - 1c =$

iv) $-s + 2s + 2 =$

v) $-7p + 4 - 3 + 6p =$

Collette can buy a soda for 0.75¢ and a bag of popcorn for 0.50¢ at the fall fair. If Collette can purchase **S** sodas and **P** bags of popcorn, then what is the meaning of the following equation?

S + **P**

NAME: ______________________

5a) On the number line below, circle 6 degrees below zero.

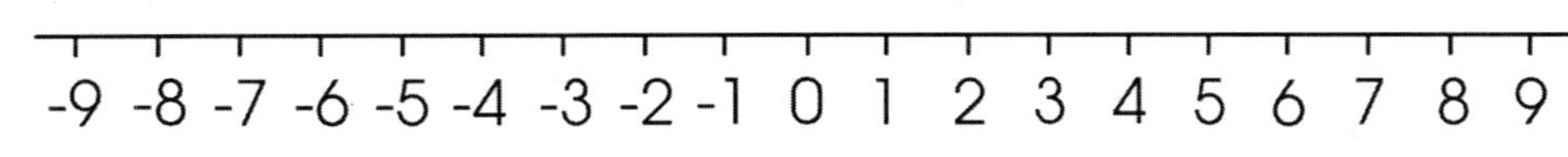

b) If the pattern below increases by the same amount, what is the seventh term in this pattern? 23, 32, 41, 50 . . . __________

c) Find each sum.

i) $(-6) + 7 =$

ii) $(-8) + (-3) =$

iii) $9 + (-3) + 2 =$

iv) $7 + (-7) + 3 + (-4) =$

v) $(-14) + (-7) + 6 =$

vi) $12 - (-4) =$

d) Rewrite using the commutative property.

i) $a + b$

ii) $5 + c$

e) What 3 items would be next in the following pattern?

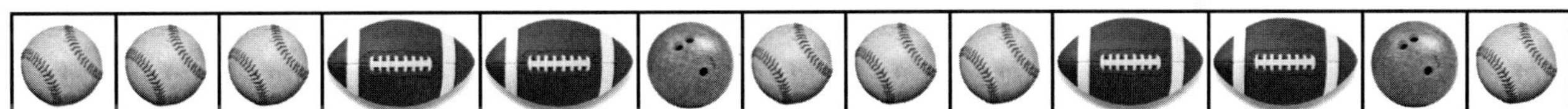

f) Solve each equation.

i) $3(4 + 2) =$

ii) $7(10 - 2) =$

iii) Let $a = 3$, $15 - a =$

iv) Let $b = -4$, $16 \div b =$

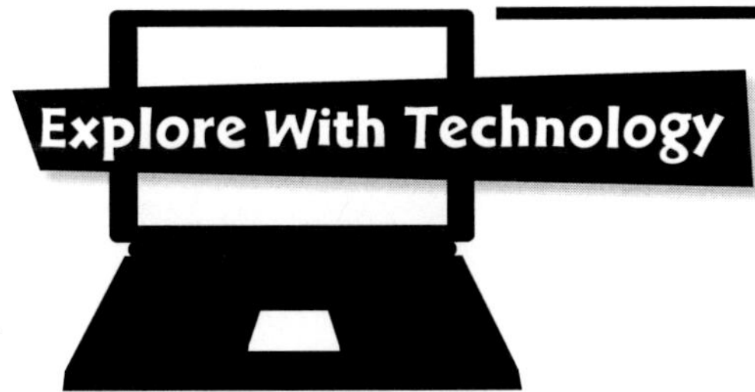

The ***Kuta Software*** site offers a great number of helpful Algebra worksheets. Visit the website, http://www.kutasoftware.com/free.html, and try some of the available algebra problems.

NAME: ______________________

6a) On the number line below, circle a profit of $3.00.

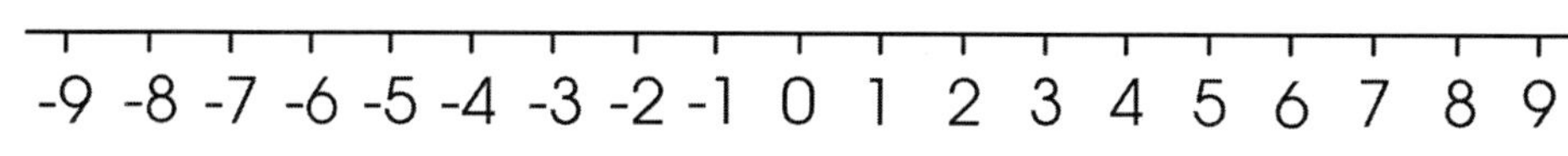

b) Rewrite using the associative property.

Ex: x + (y + z) = (x + y) + z

i) (a + b) + c

ii) d(ef)

c) Write 2 mathematical sentences using these 2 groups of lions.

____

____

d) Find each quotient.

i) −10 ÷ 5 =

ii) 6 ÷ −2 =

iii) 75 ÷ −15 =

iv) −30 ÷ 5 =

v) 22 ÷ 11 =

vi) 19 ÷ 1 =

e) Solve for a.

Ex: (2 + a) − 5 = 17
(2 + a) = 17 + 5
a = 22 − 2
a = 20

i) 12 + (a + 3) = 15 a =

ii) a − 10 = 14 a =

iii) (9 + a) + 8 = 21 a =

iv) 3(6 ÷ a) = 3 a =

v) a + 12 ÷ 4 = 11 a =

Kelly and Jake spend Saturday morning selling popcorn at the fall fair. Using the equation P = ab, calculate the money they took in (P) if ***a*** is the price of the popcorn ($2.50) and ***b*** is the number of customers (300).

Answer: ______________

NAME: ____________________

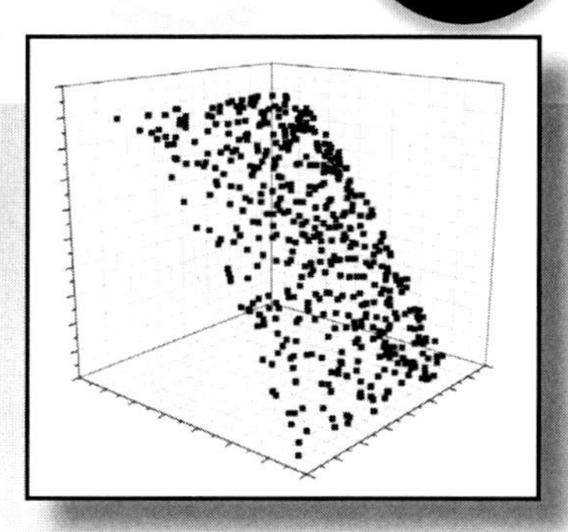

7a) Plot the following coordinates on the accompanying grid:

Ex: E = (2, 4)

A = (3, 8)

B = (6, –6)

C = (–8, 1)

D = (–4, –10)

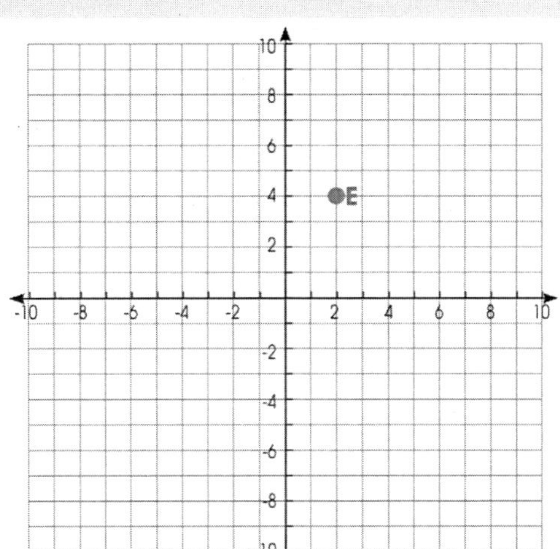

b) Rewrite the following using the distributive property.

Ex: 2 (1 + 3) = (2 × 1) + (2 × 3)

i) a(b + c) ii) 2(a + 4)

c) Graph x ≤ 5 on the number line.

-9 -8 -7 -6 -5 -4 -3 -2 -1 0 1 2 3 4 5 6 7 8 9

d) Solve the following.

i) 9 × 2 ÷ 6 =

ii) 7(3 + 2) =

iii) 3(12 ÷ 4) + 1 =

iv) 9 × 9 – 11 =

v) 10 ÷ 5(6 – 5) =

vi) 15 ÷ 3 × 4 =

vii) 16 – 4(2 + 2) =

viii) (12 – 2) + (7 × 1) =

NAME: ____________________

8a) **Graph $y \geq -7$ on the number line.**

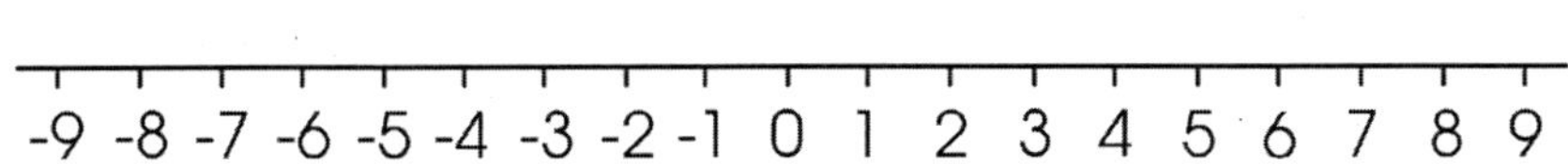

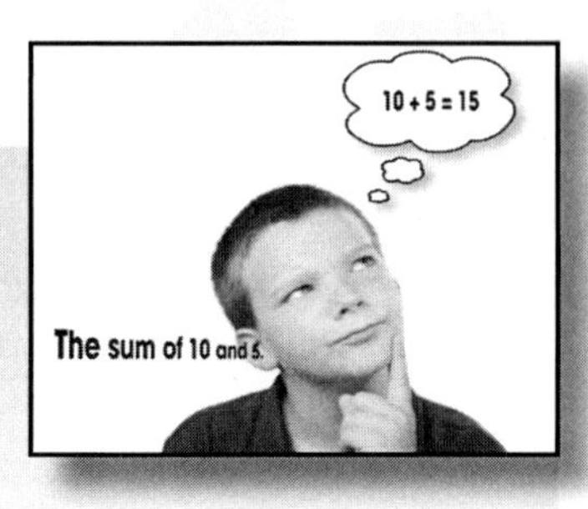

b) Write each as an algebraic expression.

i) The sum of ***b*** and 15. ________ ii) 7 squared. ________

iii) Twice ***x***. ________ iv) ***b*** cubed. ________

c) Write as a verbal expression.

i) $a \div 2 =$ ii) $5b =$

iii) $c + 8 =$ iv) $7^2 =$

d) Evaluate each expression.

i) The product of 9 and 10 ______ ii) 8 less than 15 ______

iii) 7 times 6 ______ iv) 9 squared ______

e) Which number, when placed in the box, makes the following number sentence true?

$12 - 4 \times 3 + 15 \div 5 = \square$

f) How would you show the following pattern using letters?

i. ABA ii. BAB iii. AAB iv. ABB

NAME: ______________________________

Timed Drill Sheet # 6

Minutes

9a) Continue the pattern shown in the chart below.

(1)	2	3	4	5	6	7	8	9	10
11	(12)	13	14	15	16	17	18	19	20
21	22	(23)	24	25	26	27	28	29	30
31	32	33	34	35	36	37	38	39	40
41	42	43	44	45	46	47	48	49	50

b) Evaluate these expressions.

i) $a \div 2 + b$; use $a = 2, b = 1$ ________

ii) $c + 7 \times d$; use $c = 2, d = 3$ ________

iii) $6 \times e \div f$; use $e = 6, f = 4$ ________

c) Graph $v > -7$ on the number line.

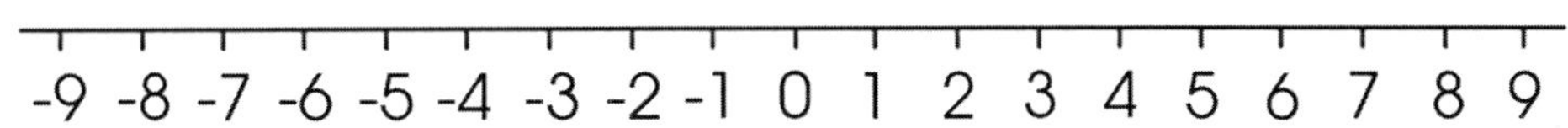

d) Write the next numbers in the following patterns.

i) 215, 245, 275, ______, ______

ii) −15, ______, −27, −33, ______

iii) − 23, −17, −11, ______, ______

iv) 7, 8, 10, 13, 17, ______, ______

e) Simplify these expressions.

i) $-12a + 7a =$

ii) $3b - b + 6b =$

iii) $5c - (-2c) =$

iv) $44d - 16d =$

v) $2e \times 2e =$

vi) $77f - (-76f) =$

NAME: ____________________

10a) Solve the following equations:

i) $2^2 =$ ii) $3^3=$ iii) $6 + 6^2 =$

iv) $3^2 + 4^2 =$ v) $12 + (2^2 + 8) =$

b) What value, when placed in the box, would make the following equation true?

$7 \times \square - 10 = 45 + 8$

c) The following pattern increases by obeying this rule: *multiply the previous term by 2 and add 3.* **6, 15, 33, 69, . . .**
What is the next term in the sequence? ________

d) Find each quotient.

i) $24 \div -6 =$ ii) $-15 \div 5 =$

iii) $-7 \div 2 =$ iv) $-14 \div 2 =$

e) Plot the following coordinates on the accompanying grid:

A = (–8, 8)

B = (0, 0)

C = (6, –7)

D = (8, 9)

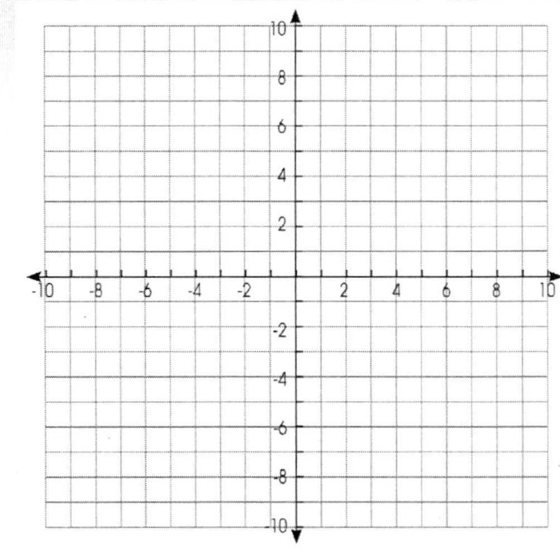

NAME: ____________________

11a) Graph $w \le 0$ on the number line.

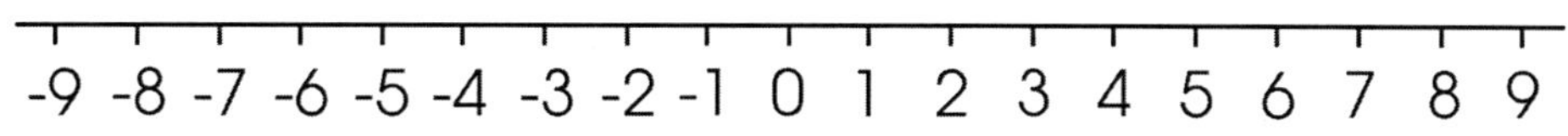

b) Evaluate each expression.

i) $a = 7$ $\quad 7 \times a + a =$ ii) $b = 4$ $\quad b \times b + b =$

iii) $c = 6$ $\quad 20 - 3 \times c =$ iv) $d = 5$ $\quad d \times d - d =$

c) How would you show the following pattern using letters?

i. ABA ii. BAB iii. AAB iv. ABB

d) Find each sum.

i) $(-9) + 12 =$

ii) $(-11) + (-11) =$

iii) $14 + 3 - (-4) + 6 =$

iv) $1 + (-2) + 13 + (-15) =$

v) $(-77) + (-21) + 50 =$

vi) $-8 + (-2 \times -4) =$

vii) $6^2 + 2(6 \div 2) =$

viii) $15 \div 5 + 6 \times 2 =$

ix) $5^3 - 124 =$

x) $-4 \times 7 + (-6) =$

Timed Drill Sheet # 8 NAME: ______________________

Minutes

12a) Which is equivalent to 3^3?

i. 81 ii. 27 iii. 63 iv. 9

b) Evaluate each using the values given.

i) $a^2 + b$; use $\boldsymbol{a} = 2$ and $\boldsymbol{b} = 3$

ii) $3c - 4d$; use $\boldsymbol{c} = 4$ and $\boldsymbol{d} = 2$

iii) $e \div f^2$; use $\boldsymbol{e} = 18$ and $\boldsymbol{f} = 3$

iv) $7g^2 \times h$; use $\boldsymbol{g} = 3$ and $\boldsymbol{h} = 1$

c) Solve for ^{a}. i) $10^a = 100$ ______ ii) $6^a = 1296$ ______

d) Write an expression for *125 reduced by a.* ______________

e) Write an expression for *the total of 66 and z.* ______________

f) Write an expression for *420 less k.* ______________

g) Rewrite using the commutative property.

i) $2y + 3z$ ii) $4a + 2b$

h) Solve the following equations.

i) 4^3 ii) 12^3

iii) 19^1 iv) 8^2

Use a calculator to complete the following. Keep in mind the proper order of operations!

$7512 + 984 \div 8 \times 17 - 108$

NAME: ______________________________

13a) What would come next in the following patterns.

i) 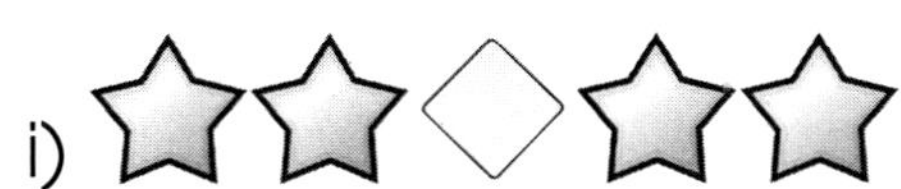 ______ ______ ______ ______

ii)  ______ ______ ______ ______

b) Find each sum.

i) (−6) + 8 =

ii) (−2) + 6 =

iii) (−8) + (−2) =

iv) (−1) + 12 + 4 =

v) 0.75 + (−2.5) =

vi) (−2.2) + (−2) − (−1.3) =

c) Graph the following by plotting the coordinates on the accompanying grid.

x	y
2	1
4	2
6	3
8	4

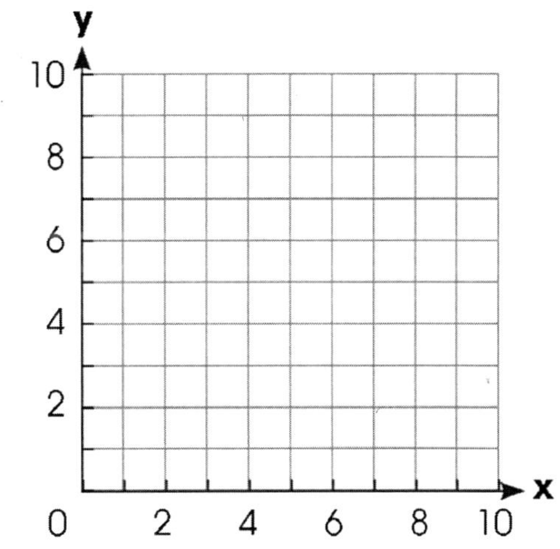

d) Find each quotient.

i) 12 ÷ 4 =

ii) −24 ÷ 12 =

iii) −10 ÷ 2 =

iv) 102 ÷ −17 =

v) 48 ÷ 8 =

vi) −72 ÷ 4 =

NAME: ______________________

14a) Continue the pattern shown in the chart below.

1	2	3	4	5	6	7	8	9	10
11	12	13	14	15	16	17	18	19	20
21	22	23	24	25	26	27	28	29	30
31	32	33	34	35	36	37	38	39	40
41	42	43	44	45	46	47	48	49	50

b) What items would be next in the following pattern?

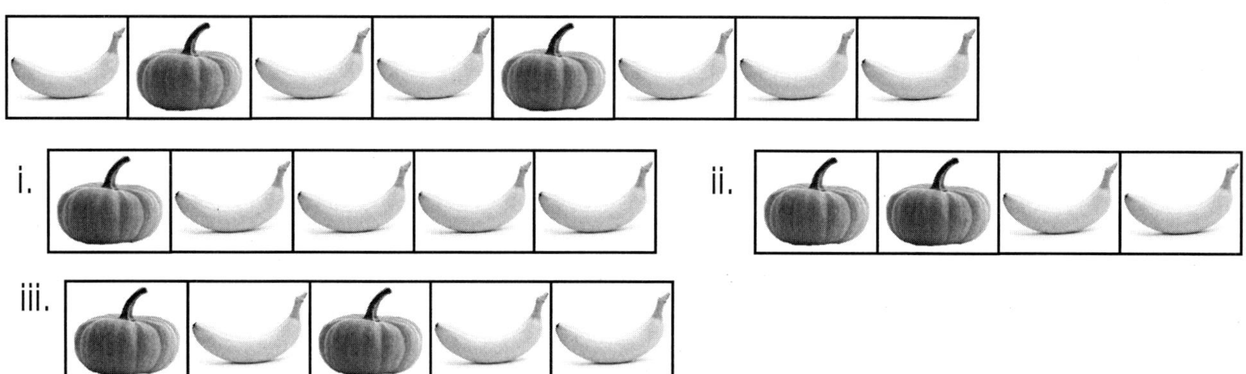

c) Simplify each expression.

Ex: $-5(x + 7) =$

$(-5 \times x) + (-5 \times 7)$

$= -5x - 35$

i) $5(2 + 8y) =$

ii) $6(-4a + 6) =$

iii) $10(-b + 9) =$

iv) $-8(7 + c) =$

v) $(3 + 7x) - 5 =$

vi) $3(-3 + x) =$

vii) $-7(-4 - d) =$

d) If a = 5, solve these equations.

i) $a + 7 =$

ii) $a(3 \times 4) =$

iii) $a^2 \div 5 =$

iv) $3a - a =$

v) $a^3 \div a =$

vi) $72 + a^2 =$

NAME: ______________________________

15a) Rewrite the equations using the associative property.

i) $(3e + 4f) + 5g$ ii) $x(yz)$

b) On the number line below, circle a loss of $7.00.

-9 -8 -7 -6 -5 -4 -3 -2 -1 0 1 2 3 4 5 6 7 8 9

c) Combine like terms.

Ex: $-5a + 6a + 2 = a + 2$

i) $4n - n =$

ii) $b - 3 - 9 =$

iii) $7y - 8 - 11 =$

iv) $-3b - 4b - b + 8 =$

v) $10 - 3(4a - 7) =$

vi) $-2(3f + 6) =$

vii) $-7t + 11t =$

d) There were 64 cows in the meadow. *c* of the cows returned to the barn. Put a checkmark beside the expression that shows how many cows remain in the field.

i. $c - 64$ ☐   ii. $64 - c$ ☐   iii. $c + 64$ ☐   iv. $c = 64$ ☐

e) Place the missing values in the box to make each equation true.

i) $14 \div \square = 10 - 3$

ii) $5^2 \times 2 = 10 \times \square$

iii) $20 \div 4 + 10 = 5 \times \square$

iv) $9 \times 9 = 60 + (7 \times \square)$

NAME: ______________________

Minutes

16a) Rewrite using the distributive property.

i) x(y + z)   ii) 5(x – 8)   iii) 4(x – y)

b) Write the missing numbers in the following patterns.

i) 88, 72, 56, _____, _____   ii) 175, _____, 205, _____, 235

c) Write each as an algebraic expression.

i) Difference of 17 and 12 _____   ii) ***b*** increased by 9 _____

iii) Product of ***c*** and 9 _____   iv) The sum of ***a*** and 21 _____

d) Evaluate each expression.

i) The product of 7 and 7 _____   ii) 6 less than 24 _____

iii) 9 times 9 _____   iv) 8 squared _____

v) Difference of 36 and 14 _____   vi) Sum of 123 and 71 _____

When painting his uncle's fence, Jeremy discovers a pattern in its construction. If he counts the number of vertical posts, subtracts 1 and multiplies by 3, he gets the number of horizontal boards. Using this information, fill in the following table.

# vertical posts	**2**	**3**	**4**	**5**	**6**
# horizontal boards					

NAME: ______________________

17a) Evaluate these expressions.

i) $a^3 + 6$, where $a = 4$ ______________________

ii) $2(16 \div b)$, where $b = 4$ ______________________

iii) $15c - 10$, where $c = 3$ ______________________

iv) $a \div b$, where $a = 15$ and $b = 3$ ______________________

v) $-12 \div c + d$, where $c = 3$ and $d = 4$ ______________________

b) Solve each equation.

Ex: $32 = 8 + a$ $\quad 32 - 8 = a$ $\quad a = 24$

i) $4 + b = 8$

ii) $16 + c = 24$

iii) $-12 + d = -8$

iv) $e + 4 = -15$

v) $f - 8 = 12$

vi) $12 = g \div 4$

vii) $-16h = -96$

viii) $i + 7 = 21$

ix) $75 - j^2 = 50$

c) Examine the input-output table shown below.

Input	Output
3	16
6	28
9	40
12	52

Which of these rules describes the data?
i. Add 15, subtract 2
ii. Multiply by 4, add 4
iii. Multiply by 5, add 1
iv. Multiply by 4, add 2

Answer: ______________________

Review Sheet

NAME: ______________________

Review A

a) Continue the pattern shown in the chart below.

1	2	3	4	5	6	7	8	9	10
11	12	13	(14)	15	16	17	18	19	(20)
21	22	23	24	25	(26)	27	28	29	30
31	32	33	34	35	36	37	38	39	40
41	42	43	44	45	46	47	48	49	50

b) Continue the following patterns.

i)   ______ ______ ______

ii) 15, 18, 21, ______, ______, ______

iii) 20, 25, 30, ______, ______, ______

iv) 9, 11, 13, 15 ______, ______, ______

v) 10, 20, 30, ______, ______, ______

c) Evaluate each expression

i) Let a = 4, 9 – a =

ii) Let b = 10, 21 + b =

iii) Let c = 5, 12 – 3 + c =

iv) Let d = 3, d × 3 =

v) Let e = 2, c + 3 – 2 =

vi) Let f = 7, f + f – 1 =

d) On the number line below, circle the number which shows five goals scored in a soccer game.

-9 -8 -7 -6 -5 -4 -3 -2 -1 0 1 2 3 4 5 6 7 8 9

e) How would you show the following pattern using letters?

i. ABA ii. BAB iii. AAB iv. ABB

f) Determine the missing members of the following number family.

7 + 3 = 10, 3 + 7 = 10 ______________ ______________

NAME: ____________________

Review B

a) Solve the following.

i) 20 – 6 = 12 + ____

ii) 11 + 7 = 8 + ____

iii) 50 – 10 = 19 + ____

iv) 50 – 35 = ____ + 10

b) Find each quotient.

i) 16 ÷ 4 =

ii) –15 ÷ 3 =

iii) 14 ÷ –7 =

c) On the number line below, circle a loss of $7.00.

-9 -8 -7 -6 -5 -4 -3 -2 -1 0 1 2 3 4 5 6 7 8 9

d) Simplify these expressions.

i) –3a + 6a =

ii) –5b + 9b – 12b =

iii) –2c + 4c + 3c =

iv) 43d – (–20d) =

e) Consider the following pattern.

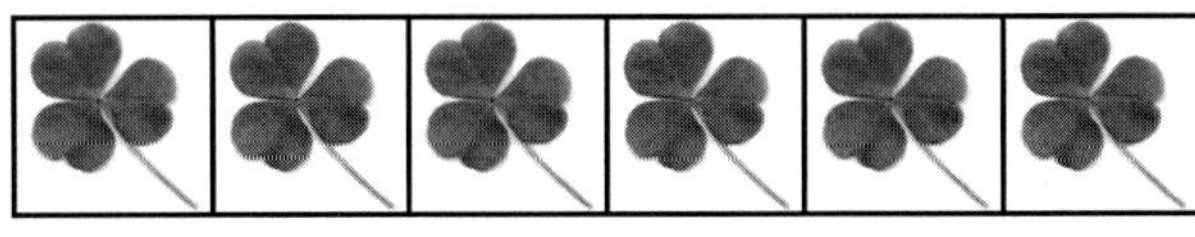

If the pattern continues in the same way, how many clovers will be in the fifth term? Answer: ____________

f) Write the next numbers in the following patterns.

i) 120, 126, 132, ____, ____

ii) –21, ____, –29, –33, ____

Review Sheet

NAME: ______________________

Review C

a) Evaluate each expression.

i) $11 + 7 \times 3 =$

ii) $16 - 12 \div 3 =$

iii) $10 \times 6 \div 3 =$

iv) $9(6 + 7) =$

v) $11 + 2(7 - 3)^2 =$

vi) $(9 + 8 + 12 - 4) \div 5 =$

b) Graph $a \leq 5$ on the number line.

-9 -8 -7 -6 -5 -4 -3 -2 -1 0 1 2 3 4 5 6 7 8 9

c) Solve for x.

i) $8 + (x + 4) = 24$, $x =$

ii) $x + 4^2 = 21$, $x =$

iii) $12 \div x = 3$, $x =$

iv) $2(6 - x) = 8$, $x =$

d) If y = 4, solve these equations.

i) $y + 12 =$

ii) $y(6 \times 2) - 4^2 =$

e) Write the missing numbers in the following patterns.

i) 99, 92, 85, ____, ____, 64

ii) −14, ____, −40, ____, ____

f) Write each as an algebraic expression.

i) Difference of 44 and 11 ______________________

ii) ***a*** increased by 22 ______________________

1.

a) $C = 25 + 2x$
$C = 25 + 2(25)$
$C = 75$

b) $C = 2.75x$
$C = 2.75 \times 25$
$C = 68.75$

c) B - by $6.25

9

2.

a)
$C = 25 + 2x$
$C = 25 + 2(50)$
$C = 125$

b) $C = 2.75x$
$C = 2.75 \times 50$
$C = 137.50$

c) A – by $12.50

d) The first option is a better deal if she rents a lot of movies.

e) i) $x + 7 = 12$
$x = 5$

ii) $13 - x = 6$
$x = 7$

iii) $7x = 42$
$x = 6$

iv) $x / 9 = 7$
$x = 63$

10

3.

a) -4 would be indicated

b) The numbers from 0 to -9 would be indicated

c) Label x at 2 and y at – 7

d) Label all numbers from -6 to 9

e) Label 4

11

4.

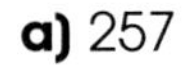

a) 257

b) 80

c) i) 647

d) Add 2 to each number

e) Add 3 to each number

f) Add 3, add 5, add 7, add 9, etc.

12

5.

a) $.75 + .80 = \$1.55$

b) $15 \times .75 = \$11.25$

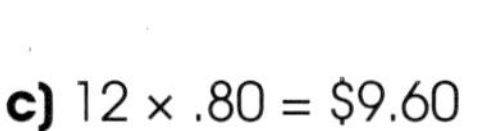

c) $12 \times .80 = \$9.60$

d) $14(.75) + 8(.80) = \$10.50 + 6.40 = \$16.90$

13

6.

3,9

5,9

9,9

1,3

14

7.

a) $x = 8$

b) $x = 6$

c) $x = 6$

d) iii) Step 3: should read
$x = 18 / 2$
so $x = 9$

e) ii) 6

15

8.

a) iv) Multiply by 2 and add 3.

b) iii) Divide by 2 and add 2.

c) 3 goals

(16)

9.

a) C = 5(250) + 2(250)
C= $1750

b) $1750 – 100 = $1650

c) Profit:

$250
$350
$300
$906
$1806

(17)

10.

a)

b)

(18)

11.

a) Store A:
C = b + xp
C = 15 + 5(2)
C = $25

Store B:
C = b + xp
C = 17.50 + 5 (1)
C = $22.50

Store B offers the better deal by $2.50.

(19)

12.

a) i) xy = 2 × 3 = 6
ii) x + y = 2 + 3 = 5
iii) y – x = 3 – 2 = 1
Therefore, i) xy has the largest value.

b) i) 6 + 2 = 8
ii) 8 – 7 = 1
iii) 21 – 8 = 13
iv) 7 + 6 = 13

c) i) -3
ii) 2

d) i) 3
ii) 16

e) i) 35
ii) 11
iii) 69

(20)

13.

a) ii) x = 2

b) iv) 3x + 5 = 2x + 7

(21)

14.

a) 11

(grows by 2 each time)

b) 21

c)

Dimes	Pennies	Total
1	.32	.42¢
2	.22	.42¢
3	.12	.42¢
4	.02	.42¢

(22)

15.

a) i) C = 2x + 4

b) Label the number 8 on the line.

c) i) x + 17 = 72
x = 55

ii) x – 43 = 12
x = 55

iii) 99 – x = 40
x = 59

d) iii) x = 18

23

Drill Sheet 1

a) i) 9
ii) 8
iii) 7
iv) 56

b) Plot 7 on the number line.

c) 241
(increases by 14)

d) i) x = 3
ii) x = 3
iii) x = 8
iv) x = 4
v) x = 96
vi) x = 8

24

Drill Sheet 2

a) 26

b) i) 10
ii) 15
iii) 16

c) 83

d) Label the numbers from – 1 to 3

25

Review A

a) i) 6
ii) 6
iii) 21
iv) 4

b) Label the number 9.

c) 28

d) iii) 2x + 2 = 1x + 3

26

Review B

a) i) x = 9
ii) x = 8
iii) x = 60

b) i) 2x - 7 = 9
ii) 4 × x = 32
iii) 3x + 1 = 25

c) Label the numbers between – 7 and 8

d) i) C = 5x + 10

e) 145

27

Review C

a) i) x = 2
ii) x = 6
iii) x = 2

b) i) 6(7) + 3(7) + 4 =
42 + 21 + 4 = 67

ii) 2(49) + 8(7) + 5 =
98 + 56 + 5 = 159

iii) 49 + 3(7) =
49 + 21 = 70

c) Label all the numbers from - 5 to 4.

d) C = f + 25x
C = 50 + 25(5)
C = 50 + 125
C = $175

e) $9.06

28

EZ✓

(these answers are for the 6 free bonus pages, see page 4 for download instructions)

1.

a) C = 4P + 6
C = 4(15) + 6
C = 60 + 6
C = 66

b) C = 4P + 6
C = 4(12) + 6
C = 48 + 6
C = 54

c) y = 3

1A

2.

a) 14 – 5 * 2 + 12 / 4 = 7

b) iv) Multiply by 3, subtract 2

c) ii) 37, 42, 47

2A

3.

a) i) x = 6 – 2
x = 4
ii) 3x = 11 – 2
3x = 9
x = 3
iii) 2x + 5 = 13
2x = 8
x = 4

b) i) Label -5 on the number line.
ii) Label all the numbers from – 9 to 5.

c) i) C = 250 + 2(12)
C = 250 + 24
C = $274
ii) C = 250 + 2(20)
C = 250 + 40
C = $290

3A

4.

3,9

2,6

9,5

7,1

4A

5.

a) i) 24

b) x + 4 = 7
~ x = 3
y + x = 5
~ y = 2
y + x + z = 10
~ z = 5

c) i) 6x – 4 – 2 =
6x = 6
x = 1
ii) 12y – 3 – 9 =
12y = 12
y = 1
iii) 3z – 1z – 4 =
2z = 4
z = 2

5A

6.

a)

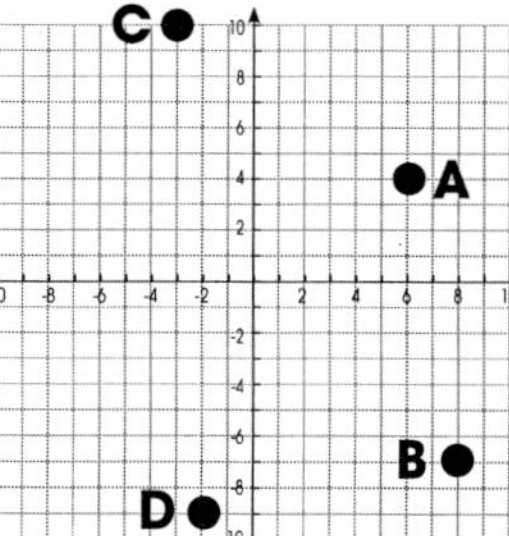
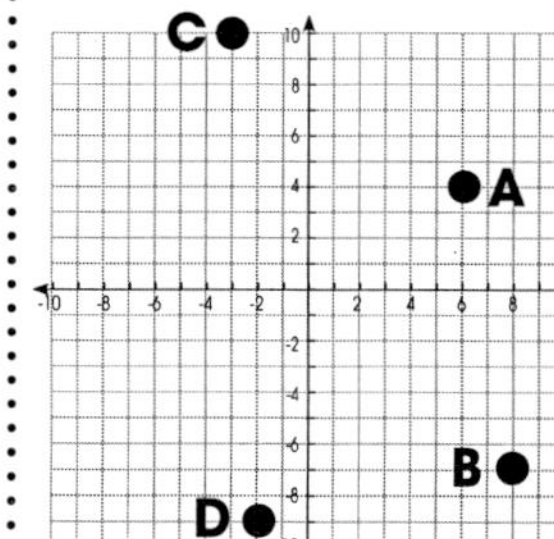

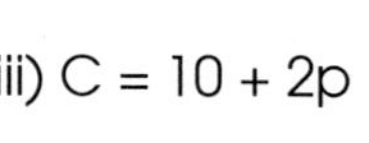

b) iii) C = 10 + 2p

c) ii)

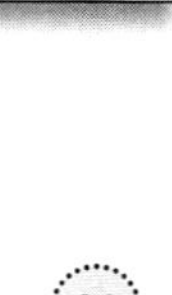

6A

1.

a)

i)

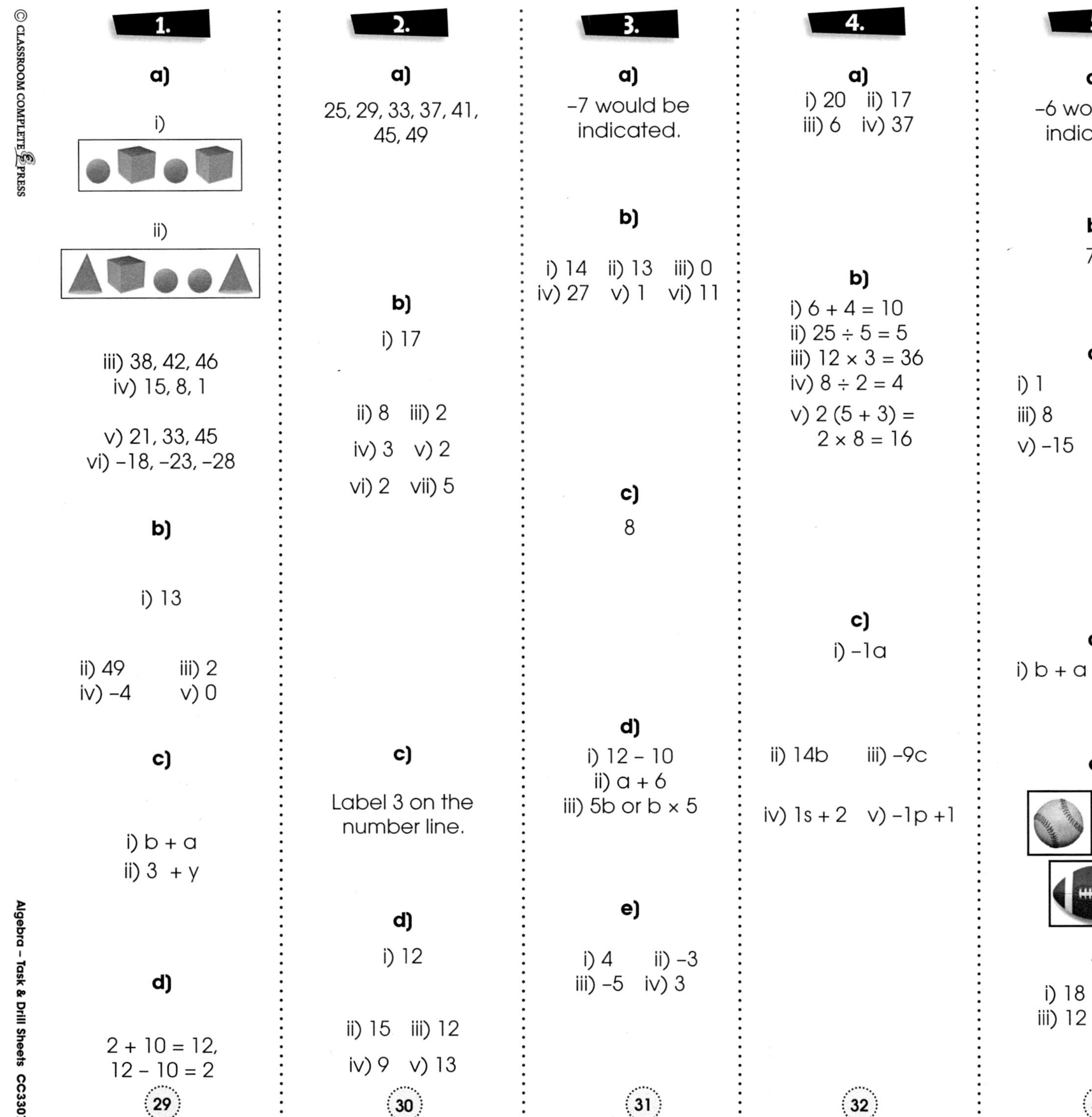

ii)

iii) 38, 42, 46
iv) 15, 8, 1

v) 21, 33, 45
vi) −18, −23, −28

b)

i) 13

ii) 49 iii) 2
iv) −4 v) 0

c)

i) b + a
ii) 3 + y

d)

2 + 10 = 12,
12 − 10 = 2

(29)

2.

a)

25, 29, 33, 37, 41, 45, 49

b)

i) 17

ii) 8 iii) 2
iv) 3 v) 2
vi) 2 vii) 5

c)

Label 3 on the number line.

d)

i) 12

ii) 15 iii) 12
iv) 9 v) 13

(30)

3.

a)

−7 would be indicated.

b)

i) 14 ii) 13 iii) 0
iv) 27 v) 1 vi) 11

c)

8

d)

i) 12 − 10
ii) a + 6
iii) 5b or b × 5

e)

i) 4 ii) −3
iii) −5 iv) 3

(31)

4.

a)

i) 20 ii) 17
iii) 6 iv) 37

b)

i) 6 + 4 = 10
ii) 25 ÷ 5 = 5
iii) 12 × 3 = 36
iv) 8 ÷ 2 = 4
v) 2 (5 + 3) = 2 × 8 = 16

c)

i) −1a

ii) 14b iii) −9c

iv) 1s + 2 v) −1p +1

(32)

5.

a)

−6 would be indicated.

b)

77

c)

i) 1 ii) −11
iii) 8 iv) −1
v) −15 vi) 16

d)

i) b + a ii) c + 5

e)

f)

i) 18 ii) 56
iii) 12 iv) −4

(33)

6.

a)

Label 3 on the number line.

b)

i) a + (b + c)
ii) (de)f

c)

Answers will vary (i.e. 6 + 4 = 10, 6 − 4 = 2)

d)

i) −2 ii) −3 iii) −5
iv) −6 v) 2 vi) 19

e)

i) a = 0

ii) a = 24 iii) a = 4
iv) a = 6 v) a = 8

(34)

EZ✓

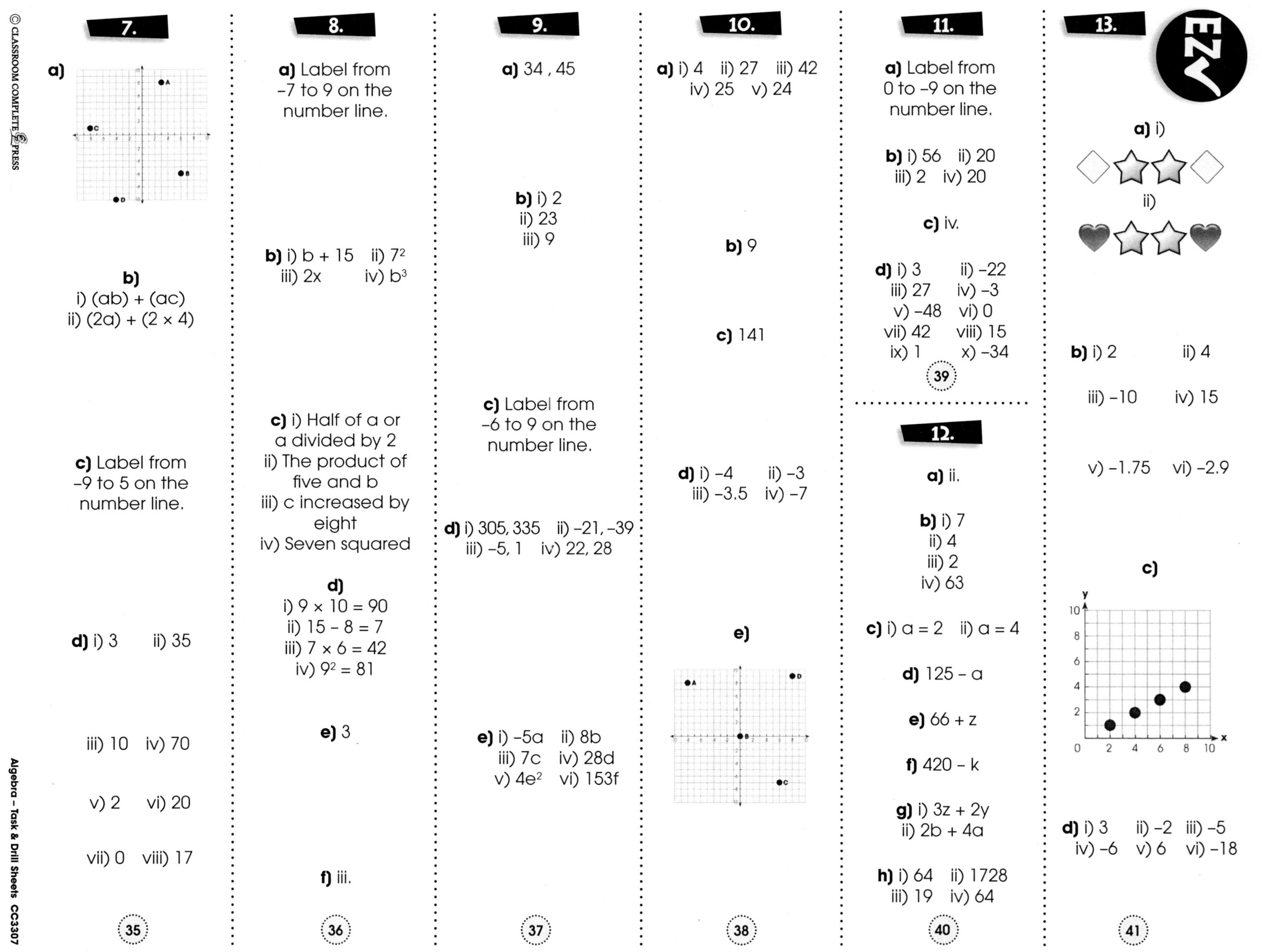

7.

a)

b)
i) (ab) + (ac)
ii) (2a) + (2 × 4)

c) Label from −9 to 5 on the number line.

d) i) 3 ii) 35
iii) 10 iv) 70
v) 2 vi) 20
vii) 0 viii) 17

35

8.

a) Label from −7 to 9 on the number line.

b) i) b + 15 ii) 7^2
iii) 2x iv) b^3

c) i) Half of a or a divided by 2
ii) The product of five and b
iii) c increased by eight
iv) Seven squared

d)
i) 9 × 10 = 90
ii) 15 − 8 = 7
iii) 7 × 6 = 42
iv) $9^2 = 81$

e) 3

f) iii.

36

9.

a) 34 , 45

b) i) 2
ii) 23
iii) 9

c) Label from −6 to 9 on the number line.

d) i) 305, 335 ii) −21, −39
iii) −5, 1 iv) 22, 28

e) i) −5a ii) 8b
iii) 7c iv) 28d
v) $4e^2$ vi) 153f

37

10.

a) i) 4 ii) 27 iii) 42
iv) 25 v) 24

b) 9

c) 141

d) i) −4 ii) −3
iii) −3.5 iv) −7

e)

38

11.

a) Label from 0 to −9 on the number line.

b) i) 56 ii) 20
iii) 2 iv) 20

c) iv.

d) i) 3 ii) −22
iii) 27 iv) −3
v) −48 vi) 0
vii) 42 viii) 15
ix) 1 x) −34

39

12.

a) ii.

b) i) 7
ii) 4
iii) 2
iv) 63

c) i) a = 2 ii) a = 4

d) 125 − a

e) 66 + z

f) 420 − k

g) i) 3z + 2y
ii) 2b + 4a

h) i) 64 ii) 1728
iii) 19 iv) 64

40

13.

EZ✓

a) i)

ii)

b) i) 2 ii) 4
iii) −10 iv) 15
v) −1.75 vi) −2.9

c)

d) i) 3 ii) −2 iii) −5
iv) −6 v) 6 vi) −18

41